62660

6/he

CANADA

Nina Nelson

CANADA

B. T. Batsford Ltd *London*

To the memory of my father
Claude Noonan
who took me on my first travels

First published 1980
© Nina Nelson 1980

ISBN 0 7134 1841 9

Photoset by Progress Typesetting
Printed and bound in Great Britain by
Redwood Burn Ltd, Trowbridge & Esher
for the publishers
B. T. Batsford Ltd, 4 Fitzhardinge Street, London W1H 0AH

CONTENTS

ILLUSTRATIONS

ACKNOWLEDGMENTS

I wish to express my gratitude to members of the Canadian Government Office of Tourism for their help while in Canada. In particular I owe special thanks to Tom Hill, their representative in London, who had helpful suggestions, assisted with plans and remained unruffled however often they were changed. Special thanks also to Jane Whigham of Stuart Hulse Associates who enthusiastically worked out an itinerary which covered as many tourist 'musts' as possible. Tom and Jane helped check this manuscript and any remaining mistakes are my own. If they did not know the answers to my queries they always found someone who did. It is also a pleasure to work with my editor at Batsford, Paula Shea, whose understanding of the problems of a travel writer is something all too rare nowadays.

I had unstinted help from the people I met on my travels across Canada and I must mention Lorraine Cooper of the Visitor Information Centre in Victoria who not only showed us the island but also introduced us to Miracle. Also Jean Anderson and Edra McLeod of the Vancouver Convention and Visitors Bureau for showing us round their city and pointing out many things we should otherwise have missed.

In Calgary, Al Bailey of their Tourist and Convention Association stampeded us around, and his boss Doug Johnson reckoned we needed white stetsons. In Toronto it was Bill Holtzmann of the Metropolitan Convention and Tourist Bureau who did everything but get us through the eye of the needle. We saw Winnipeg according to Cory Kilvert, an experienced hand with a feeling for his city. The flavour of Montreal was encapsulated by Gilles Gosselin, and Bobby Goyer showed us the Laurentians. Ottawa came alive with the enthusiasm of Claude Lachaine while Quebec's old-world charm was lovingly demonstrated by Theo Maskis. Further east Helen Jean Newman of Tourism New Brunswick showed us Fredericton, while Nova Scotia Department of Tourism's Sharon Martin had a zest for Halifax which was infectious. Doug Wheeler reminisced effectively in Newfoundland.

On the friends and relatives front Jean Danard, travel editor of the Toronto Financial Post, gave great encouragement; Lucy and Andy Anderson my sister and brother-in-law, shared their encyclopaedic knowledge of the Annapolis Valley and in Newfoundland, life-long friends Olga and Lewis Ayre helped to bring the scenes of my childhood flooding back and gave us a memorable visit to Gander and Grand Falls. Lord Alexander of Tunis kindly offered to make his father's papers available for research.

Of the many hotels and restaurants which we visited, Brian Lilley, manager of Chateau Lake Louise, had a real feel for his profession.

Michael Broadhurst of the Banff Springs Hotel ably backed up by Audrey de Baghy, ran a tight ship. Anita Wagenaar of the Vancouver Sheraton Landmark ably demonstrated the facilities at our disposal and Marie Brancolini almost caused my delectable meal at La Sapinière to get cold in her keenness to cover her subject.

Finally my deepest thanks to Marie Chitty who somehow found time during a short holiday to type the manuscript.

The author and publishers would like to thank the following for the use of their prints: Douglas Dickins, 1, 4, 5, 8, 9, 10, 12, 13 and 17; Department of Public Relations, Vancouver, 3; Canadian Government Office of Tourism, 6; CP Hotels, 7; Department of Public Relations, City of Montreal, 14, 15 and 16; Parks Canada, 20 and 21; and the New Brunswick Department of Tourism, 22. Photos 2, 11, 18 and 19 are from the author's collection.

The maps were drawn by Anthony Nelson.

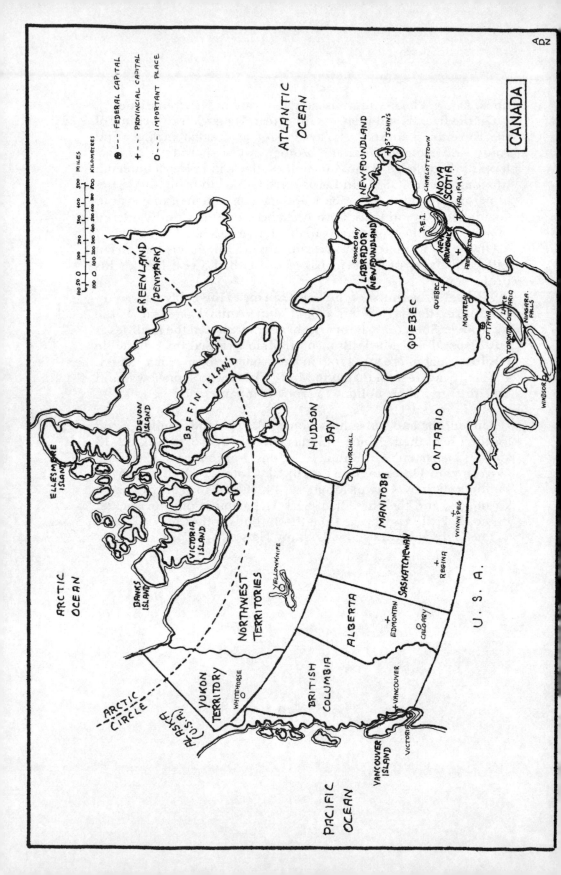

1 CANADA TODAY AND YESTERDAY

Even for the visitor who has travelled widely, the first thing that is different about Canada is its sheer size. Stretching between the Pacific and the Atlantic it could easily contain the whole of Europe. The distances, the time and climatic changes are almost overwhelming, especially when you remember the unrelenting struggles of tiny Holland to reclaim land from the sea. You cannot avoid contrasting the overflow of miniscule Hong Kong onto the sea itself, or the comparative population density of England with the abundance of space in this, the second largest country in the world. Incredible to realize that the Trans-Canada-Highway is the longest continuous road on earth — over 5,000 miles (8,000 kilometres) in length. It is only when you learn that the St Lawrence river drains a territory of 500,000 square miles (1,295,000 square kilometres) which contains half the fresh water in the world, that you begin to comprehend Canada's vastness. The country spans seven time zones.

The very provinces seem like countries in themselves. British Columbia stretches from the Pacific to the Rockies. Alberta borders the Rockies on the other side, which themselves dwarf the Alps. Ontario with its half million square miles, Quebec where whole areas have yet to be explored. The immeasurable prairies of Manitoba and Saskatchewan, not forgetting the Maritimes; Nova Scotia snatched from the French; New Brunswick founded by the Loyalists; Prince Edward Island one of the richest farming communities known and Newfoundland, unique in that it is the youngest province yet was the first to be discovered. The Northwest Territories with their large potential resources are still a mystery and just becoming of tourist interest.

Perhaps the most exciting thing about Canada is that although it seems to be several countries in one, the size is minimized by excellent transport systems. If cities do not appeal and you want peace and quiet to 'get away from it all' there is plenty of room to do so and everybody does. The claim of Manitoba's Whiteshell Provincial Park that, 'Solitude and respite are never further away than round the bend of a river in the lee of a rock bound island,' is true—not only there but in the thousands of square miles of other provincial parks. As for sportsmen there is something for every type of angler from the boy with his worm-baited hook to the lavishly equipped deep-sea fisherman. An old friend of mine whose hobby is salmon fishing finds it cheaper and more rewarding to go to Newfoundland for this, even including the return passage, than to rent a stream in Scotland.

There is much that is refreshingly different in Canada. Overtaxed as most of us are today, it comes as a pleasant surprise to learn that Alberta needs to levy no provincial taxes, due to the revenue it obtains from its oil. With the movement of most goods only possible at the expenditure of considerable energy, how satisfying to watch on occasions half-a-mile-long rafts of timber carried effortlessly and silently to their destination by swirling rivers.

The history of Canada is a saga of man's adventurous spirit, with the French and British struggling to out do each other in their efforts to open up the country and harness its resources. It is still wide open to the pioneer and entrepreneur.

During Henry VII's reign John Cabot sailed in a small ship from Bristol to seek a 'new world'. The King gave him a charter in return for which John Cabot, who was not English but a Venetian navigator, was to give the King one fifth of any diamonds, gold or other treasure that he might find in a distant country. Cabot left in May 1497 and returned in July saying he had planted a large cross on the shore of a new land he had discovered which he imagined was near Japan. The King awarded him ten golden guineas for the 'New Found Land'. There is a mural depicting this event on one of the walls in London's Houses of Parliament. This discovery tempted Henry to explore further and he sent Cabot off again next year with two ships. This time he returned with tales, not of oriental treasures, but of wealth in a different form. The coastline around Newfoundland literally shelved into the Atlantic and the shallow waters stretched far out from the land and was a breeding ground for a profusion of cod, salmon and lobster. So began the era of the 'Fishing Admirals', and the island's records, laws and traditions have had a nautical flavour ever since.

These early sailors followed a makeshift plan each year which worked fairly well. The captain of the first ship to arrive at the fishing grounds was 'Admiral' for the season, the second was 'Vice Admiral' and the third 'Rear Admiral'. In later years came naval controllers and their deputies who eventually gave place to governors. The latter were required to have sea in their veins and were usually retired naval officers who only spent the fishing season in the island — until in 1825 when the first resident governor was appointed.

In 1534 Jacques Cartier sailed from France on a similar mission to that of John Cabot to find the orient and return laden with gems, spices and gold. He discovered the Gulf of St Lawrence and his commercial reward was not gold but furs. Another Frenchman, Samuel de Champlain, founded the first white settlement at Annapolis Royal in 1605 and three years later, a second one which became Quebec city.

Consequent upon the wars and treaties in Europe, the English and French granted and relinquished to each other great tracts of Canada but, as in other countries, it was left to a commercial enterprise, The Hudson's Bay Company, to do much of the opening up. Even today this great organization still serves some three hundred communities.

An English navigator, Henry Hudson, was never to know that his name would go down in history. He sailed on behalf of the Muscovy and Dutch East India Companies and discovered the river and the gigantic bay which were named after him. Sadly, on his last Canadian voyage his crew mutinied, set him adrift in a small boat with his son and a few loyal sailors with no food or water. He was never seen again.

In 1610 Charles II granted a charter to Prince Rupert, his cousin, and seventeen other influential noblemen of the day including the Duke of Marlborough, to trade with the Indians for furs. The company's name was a stirring one: 'The Governor and Company of Adventurers Trading into Hudson's Bay'. The Charter gave the company consent to barter with Indian tribes whose settlements were watered by streams flowing into Hudson Bay. This covered enormous territory and rival fur traders, especially the French, did not take kindly to this idea. The sacking and burning of forts and skirmishes to the death were commonplace. Despite this, Prince Rupert's company survived and toughened. Its fame grew as it opened up new territories. Their chief rivals were the North West Fur Company of Montreal who finally joined them in 1821.

A few years later negotiations between the company and the new Federation of Canada gave the former £300,000 in exchange for a 'fertile belt' bounded as follows. 'On the south by the US boundary, on the west by the Rocky Mountains, on the north by the northern branch of the Saskatchewan river, on the east by Lake Winnipeg, the Lake of Woods, and the waters connecting them.' The Hudson's Bay Company retained one twentieth part of their original holdings and 45,000 acres of land adjacent to the company's trading posts. All in all it suited both parties.

It seems strange today when wild animals are assiduously protected, that their slaughter should have carried on so long unabated and brought such wealth to Europe. France and Russia were close on the heels of the British and the fur trade continued to be big business during the 1800s and early 1900s—even today trapping on a small scale is lucrative in places like Alberta and the north generally.

In those far away days there was little warmth in clothing or dwellings. No such things existed as central heating, double glazing, wall-to-wall carpeting or indeed man-made fibres of any kind. Canadian furs meant warmth in every sense of the word. They were beautiful, pliable and silky to the touch. They were adaptable for bed and floor coverings, not to mention clothing. Besides the popular beaver there were bear skins and fox furs of excellent quality, not only brown and red, but white from the polar regions.

For over three hundred years the Hudson's Bay Company has thrived. Its fur auctions are world famous, but it has diversified its business into other things such as oil and merchandising. It has offices or shops all over the country. Its large departmental stores sell everything from caviar to Brussels lace. An offer of £151,700,000 was made by Lord Thomson, another Canadian, owner of the London Times, for its department store chain in 1979. What would Henry Hudson have thought of that!

To return to the early days of wrangling between the French and the English over the possession of the land: Champlain settled in Quebec with twenty-seven colonists in 1608 and remained there until his death twenty years later. After him as governor came the Comte de Frontenac. Champlain had been content with farming and trading but the Comte created a small city and held court with the ceremony expected of a representative of Louis XIV. French ships arrived with handsome furniture and clothing for this tiny oasis of refinement, and much attention was paid to the social life of the colony. Frontenac fell out with Laval, the Bishop of Quebec, who also held jurisdiction over all the French in the country, and was against trading liquor with the Indians. On this vexed question the Comte wished merely to control its distribution. This dispute did nothing to quell the disquiet of the local Iroquois Indians who were restless under French rule and harried them with intermittent raids. Frontenac, jealous of authority, was firm with his own people and his severity affected the settlers and became proverbial. In the meantime the British had founded Halifax and were opening up Nova Scotia.

When the Seven Years' War started in Europe it decided much of Canada's fate, and also that of the district known in Nova Scotia and New Brunswick as Acadia, where French citizens who had kept their allegiance to France were harshly deported. It also brought to the fore a new English Major General — James Wolfe — who was sent on an expedition across the Atlantic to Quebec. The French were warned and under the command of the Marquis de Montcalm waited on the high ridge of cliffs overlooking the St Lawrence river to repel the invader.

Wolfe, on a previous foray across the Atlantic, had by means of a ruse already taken the fort and town of Louisbourg at the entrance of the Gulf of St Lawrence. Knowing the French in Quebec thought their high cliffs were well nigh impregnable he decided on a similar plan. Wolfe took his small army in boats by night along the St Lawrence and stealthily effected a landing at a place now known as Wolfe's Cove. The battle was fought on land edging the top of the cliffs known as the Plains of Abraham for no better reason than that it belonged to a wealthy farmer by the name of Abraham. At dawn an astonished General Montcalm found himself facing Wolfe and his men. Desperate fighting took place but the surprise tilted victory toward the British and Wolfe wrested Quebec from Montcalm. Both leaders were mortally wounded during the battle.

It is said that Wolfe quoted Grey's 'elegy' before the action, pausing at the lines 'The paths of glory lead but to the grave.' In Quebec's Battlefields Park there is a column bearing the words: 'Here died Wolfe victorious on the 13th September 1750.' In the Governor's garden there is another memorial to Wolfe but this he shares with his adversary. The simple inscription reads: 'Wolfe and Montcalm'. Yet a third memorial to Wolfe is in Westminster Abbey.

When the Treaty of Paris was signed after the Seven Years' War, France relinquished her claims in Canada save for the two small islands of St Pierre and Miquelon, off Newfoundland. They are still part of France today. Henceforward Canada was ruled from Britain by Royal Proclamation. French Roman Catholics enjoyed freedom of worship and retained their own customs, and French and British civil law were practised side by side. This seemingly blissful state of affairs was interrupted in 1775 by American colonists who were very irate at King George III's taxes. They invaded Canada hoping the French Canadians would join them. Montreal fell and Quebec withstood a bitter seige. When they withdrew over the border some forty thousand American loyalists fled to Canada. They were not permitted by the Americans to bring any money or belongings, but England recognized their claims and sent some £400,000 to rehabilitate them. They settled mostly in Ontario, Nova Scotia and New Brunswick.

The first properly organized white settlement in Manitoba was begun by Gaultier de Varennes when he built Fort Rouge in 1738 at the junction of the Red and Assiniboine rivers. Later Lord Selkirk arrived with settlers from the Scottish Highlands and from these beginnings grew Winnipeg — but not without bloodshed.

Sometime before the French and British forts had been built the Metis had been hunting, fishing and trapping sporadically. They were of mixed French and Indian blood and led a rough kind of utopian existence with small farms running down to the rivers. They bitterly resented the newcomers and felt it threatened their way of life. One of their teachers, Louis Riel, headed a revolt. This rebellion was soon crushed. In 1870 Manitoba joined the Dominion. In 1873 Prince Edward Island did likewise.

British Columbia came into the fold in 1871 on the understanding that a transcontinental railway would be built. By 1885 the Canadian Pacific Railway was completed — a tremendous task. Alberta and Saskatchewan joined the other provinces having been formed from the Northwest Territories. Newfoundland became the tenth province as recently as 1949.

The title 'Royal Canadian Mounted Police' is as famous as that of the 'Hudson's Bay Company' although the Mounties were formed a couple of centuries later. Their exploits and devotion to duty, often under conditions of great hardship, are legendary. Even those who know little about Canada recognize them in pictures with their vivid red tunics, broad-rimmed hats and often on parade with their splendid horses. The Mounties were founded in 1873, a carefully selected band of three hundred men. They were an organization created to keep law and order, neither strictly a police force nor a military unit but something in between. One of their main jobs was to keep peace between the settlers and the Indians.

It was an understood thing that the Hudson's Bay Company never traded liquor with the Indians, but other traders were not so particular. The Mounties had to clear up many 'Whiskey Forts' which bartered the worst kind of 'Moonshine' with the Indians, making them literally fighting mad. Trading also went on from over the border and the US Cavalry sometimes trespassed onto Canadian soil to quell the Indians. The Mounties seldom ran into the same trouble. Perhaps this is best explained by a well-known story.

An Indian tribe which had crossed into Canada to escape the wrath of some traders, were finally persuaded to return to their own land with the new promise of no reprisals. They were led to the border by two Mounties, the senior of whom was a sergeant. On arrival at the boundary they were met by an escort of American cavalry. The colonel rode forward and the Mountie sergeant approached to greet him. 'Where is your regiment?' asked the colonel. 'Oh,' said the Mountie giving a smart salute, 'he is back there with the Indians!'

The Canadian Indians fared better than their American cousins largely due to the Mounties and also reasonably fair dealings with the traders. However, their contact with the whites exposed them to diseases against which they had built up no immunity and many contracted tuberculosis, syphilis and other contagious illnesses, more often than not with fatal results. They also took readily to alcohol to which their normal diet did not adapt them and this too often led to tragic consequences, and still does.

The Indians are not a single race and the tribes have different characteristics. Treaties were made with some of them during the opening up of the country; others were hostile, especially when the railway was being built. They believed that spirits dwelt in such things as waterfalls, rivers and trees; visions and magic powers were taken seriously. Like the ancient Egyptians they thought that the dead must be buried with many of their earthly goods to accompany them to the next world and that the ghosts of the dead helped the living. They supposed that man consisted of three parts: body, spirit and soul. Christianity was accepted by many quite naturally. One of their most interesting beliefs concerns the tree of life, which is a great tree stretching skyward, its roots being of different tribes. An eagle is perched on the top keeping guard, its eyes fearless of the sun—again like the ancient Egyptians' Horus, the divine hawk. You sometimes see a carved eagle on top of a totem pole.

Perhaps the story of the Blackfoot is the most appealing. Although proud, their famous chief Crowfoot saw the writing on the wall when the white man came. Rather than sacrifice his people with no hope whatever of victory over the intruder, he salvaged what he could for them and gave in with dignity. The Blackfoot were great warriors known as the 'Tigers of the Plain'. There was no need to prove their worth. Crowfoot knew the days of the buffalo were numbered. He knew that the white man had come to stay and felt that he must get the best deal he could for his tribe and then put the future of his people into the hands of the newcomer. Today those Indians who have not mingled with the other Canadians live on tracts of land known as 'reserves' and their affairs are looked after by the Federal Indian Affairs and Northern Development Department.

The building of the Canadian Pacific Railway which began in 1871 was hazardous to say the least. It cost a fortune and its construction faced the most appalling engineering problems. At one stage bankruptcy nearly put an end to it. An amazing character, William Cornelius Van Horne, saved the day by convincing Sir John MacDonald, the Prime Minister, that to give up the railway would be to relinquish Canada itself. London banks were urged to provide more and more money—which they did. Sometimes more than 3 miles (5 kilometres) of rails could be laid in a day across the prairies where the going was easy. However, blasting a way through the Rockies was quite another matter and even today, the Kicking Horse Pass which climbs to 5,000 feet (1,500 metres), takes your breath away.

Pictures of Van Horne show him as a tall man of tremendous girth with a beard and waxed moustache and a determined expression. One of his sayings is reputed to have been, 'I eat all I can, I drink all I can and I don't give a damn for anyone.'

Nova Scotia and New Brunswick helped to found Canada in 1867 and British Columbia agreed to join the Federation in 1871 on the understanding that a transcontinental railway should be built immediately the deal went through. Railways were at that time the fastest way of travel and quite elaborate systems linked even out-of-the-way villages. Two new systems came into being, the Canadian Northern and the Grand Trunk Pacific. These failed financially so they amalgamated and became state-owned—the Canadian National Railway. It was known as the CN, and the Canadian Pacific Railway as the CP. Due to the fact that about half the population live within 200 miles (320 kilometres) north of the American border the two railways duplicate each other and there has always been a friendly rivalry between them and this close competition has given Canadians choices and the best of services.

Nowadays the railways have a hard time of it from the passenger aspect, being unable to compete with air services covering the whole country—not to mention fast long-distance coach networks with stations in all the main towns. It seems strange that railway stations are often no longer in the cities. The decline in passenger traffic no longer justifies the expense of maintaining a downtown station. However, a Crown Corporation has now been formed to operate the combined passenger services of CN and CP under the name VIA, just as the Americans have done with Amtrak, in order to try to win back passenger traffic. If this proves successful some city terminals may be re-opened but meanwhile it pays to be selective about the use of train travel. There is still a daily train run through the Rockies which is a unique experience viewed from one of the dome observation cars. Mention must also be made of the daily high-speed service between Toronto and Montreal. The railways seem to hold their own for freight purposes however and it is a memorable sight for European eyes to see trains of a hundred and fifty huge cars often hauled by three or four engines, winding their way along the tracks.

As in America, the car is an essential part of the Canadian way of life. Excellent freeways and roads link towns and cities and there seem to be fewer traffic jams than in Europe. This is not only because of space but is a spin-off from the arrangement of most towns on the grid principle of road layout. A cross reference of numbers, letters or names in alphabetical order, makes navigation much easier and traffic flow is less interrupted by drivers hesitating and stopping while trying to find their way.

Driving is of course on the right side of the road and gasoline (petrol) prices vary from province to province but are always cheaper than in Europe. A switch over from gallons to litres is being made. There are also inter-provincial variations in the wearing of seat belts and the application of speed limits which must be watched carefully. These are often enforced in the busy season by air patrols who measure the car's speed by timing it across a grid of lines on the road and radio to police cars to catch the unwary. I must admit that our observance of the limits as visitors often meant that we were endlessly overtaken. Distances are now marked in kilometres and the only tolls on motorways are for bridges and on the Laurentian autoroute in Quebec.

One thing which will strike the visitor is the large amount of 'campers' to be seen all across Canada but especially in the western provinces. In the east people seem to prefer summer cottages or fishing shacks. 'Campers' appears to be a general term applied to any type of vehicle from a small trailer caravan to a palatial motor home 40 or more feet (12 metres) long. Everybody seems ready to 'take off' and enjoy themselves at weekends or on holiday to the provincial parks or a favourite lake or mountain, while bringing many of their creature comforts with them. There are some trailer caravans ranging from the small, collapsible two-berth model to the large aluminium railway-carriage type. Then come the smaller motor homes often mounted on a pick-up truck and provided with jacks so that they can be dismounted at home or on a camp site, leaving the truck available for normal use.

Finally you will see many larger motor homes on purpose-built chassis ranging in length from about 20 to 50 feet (6-15 metres). These are the most luxurious and can provide a permanent home for two, four or six people, often retired, who move south into America in the winter and return to Canada in the summer. They provide every facet of normal living, running hot and cold water with shower, bath and flushing lavatory, gas cooker, refrigerator, deep freeze, television, air conditioning and even telephone. You can pull into a campsite offering 'hook ups' and plug into mains electricity, fill your water tank, empty your sewage tank and recharge your gas bottles as well as buy your groceries.

'Campers' offer a whole new way of life and several British travel companies are now offering a package comprising a flight out and back and hire of a camper for four to six people or a family with children, which is very good value for money. Even the bigger motor homes are not difficult to drive with power steering, brakes and automatic gears but I was asked several times to go back and sit on the lavatory seat when my husband was backing out of a site and tell him what he was going to hit! Typical refinements which we often saw were cross-country motor cycles hanging in racks at the back of the motor home and cars towed behind on rigid tow bars for use on arrival at the destination.

Driving and drinking never intermarry and you can lose your licence for this offence as quickly as in any other country. The laws on drinking differ from province to province and some seem strange to us. For instance it is stricter with women than with men. New Brunswick and Quebec forbid them to enter taverns. It is the same in Nova Scotia but they are allowed in what are called 'cocktail lounges'. However they are permitted to enter taverns in Newfoundland and Alberta which is said to have the most reasonable liquor prices. In Manitoba and Saskatchewan mixed company drinking is legal everywhere over the age of eighteen. Some Ontario communities frown on liquor. In Prince Edward Island liquor stores are not always open. The rules change as you cross the country and it is impossible to remember them all.

We found that the best thing to do was to enquire about the local regulations at our hotel. On Sundays in many places a drink is only allowed with meals. One evening we were going by train from Kenora to Sudbury and watching a truly gorgeous sun set. I thought it would be nice to have a glass of sherry before going to the dining car for dinner. I was amazed when a passing waiter said we could not do so. It is mildly annoying that there are no wine merchants as such and you can only buy alcohol at provincial 'liquor stores' which are often extremely difficult to find, though you can buy beer in grocery stores in Quebec. In addition you are limited to what they choose to stock and the ordinary working of supply and demand does not operate. If ever we asked a passerby where to find one he or she always seemed to be a teetotaller!

Several national holidays are like our own, such as Christmas Day, Good Friday, Easter Monday and Remembrance Day. New Year's Day is a holiday and there is Victoria Day on the nearest Monday to 24 May, when there are fireworks' displays across the country. Others are Dominion Day, 1 July, Labour Day the first Monday in September and Thanksgiving Day the second Monday in October. Often if a holiday falls on a Saturday or Sunday it is observed on the following Monday. Besides these holidays there are several provincial ones. Seasonal events also differ from province to province.

Detailed statements about the weather are difficult to make in a country of this size. Temperatures are given in Celsius. In general, autumns are crisp, winter cold often with snow, summers warm to hot and spring arrives late in the Maritimes and is brief. There are no particular health hazards and patent medicines are easy to obtain although it is advisable to bring your own specialized prescription. For instance, I suffer from migraine and find one certain brand cures it and these tablets I can buy from any chemist's shop in England but, as they contain a little codeine which is on prescription in Canada, I cannot buy them over the counter.

Tourist guidance is arranged on a provincial basis, often delegated down to cities, towns and areas. Excellent maps, guide books and accommodation lists are readily available and most offices will go out of their way to help the visitor, especially when fully manned in the tourist season.

The Canadians you meet, perhaps relatives, friends of friends or business acquaintances, accept you immediately and their hospitality can be overwhelming. They still retain the community spirit of the old frontier days. If they find you are not their cup of tea you will be dropped then and there. Perhaps this is a better way of receiving people than our artificial way of keeping our distance when we meet someone until we see whether we are going to like him. But then this is borne of necessity to maintain some privacy in a densely populated small island. On the other hand if you are a loner and want to do things by yourself you will be left to your own devices and there is plenty of room for you. Nobody tries to impress you with the amount of work he does or the importance of his own particular town.

The average Canadian is proud of tradition but progressive. He can explain the idiosyncrasies of the American to the Britisher and that of the Britisher to the American because he himself is a mixture of both. His way of life tends to be very much like that of the American materially but he has retained many of the customs and manners of his British, French and European forbears.

In the early days Canada was invaded several times by the Americans and retaliated. Fierce skirmishes resulted, including the burning down of part of Toronto and the reprisal raid on Washington where the White House was set on fire. Today, unlike the troubles in Ireland, all is forgiven and forgotten and the two countries pursue a good-neighbour policy.

Canadians came to Britain's aid in 1914, leaving their families and businesses behind. On sea, land and in the air they more than made their mark. Their bravery and courage at Vimy Ridge and Ypres are not forgotten even today. At Ypres each evening traffic through the Menin Gate is halted and it is a time when the allies of those far off days are remembered. Buglers, recruited from the local fire brigade, sound the 'Last Post' and everything is silent. Only during the Second World War was this nightly ritual interrupted. At the end of the war on the first night of Ypres' liberation, the 'Last Post' rang out from beneath the Menin Gate once more even before the remnants of the enemy had left the town. Also at Ypres the Canadians are especially remembered at 'Sanctuary Wood' where a long avenue of maple trees has been planted in memoriam.

During the Second World War the sons of the men who fought at Vimy Ridge and Ypres showed that they were made of the same valiant stuff as their fathers, this time particularly in Holland at Nijmegen. Here you can visit the beautifully kept Canadian War Cemetery some 6 miles (10 kilometres) south at Groesbeek, on a hill above the battlefield, where they fought so tenaciously. There are over a thousand Canadian graves.

Another major contribution in the Second World War was the

flying training programme. This produced thousands of Allied air crews much more rapidly than would have been possible in the United Kingdom where weather, shortage of airfields and enemy interference would have made it impossible. Since that time Canada has always been ready to lend its forces to the United Nations peace-keeping operations and units have seen service in the Middle East and elsewhere.

Freedom of worship is scrupulously observed and social life is often centred around the churches. These buildings are so contrasting that they add to the charm of cities like Winnipeg where onion-shaped domes on Ukrainian churches mix with ornate Gothic spires and steeples and the simple towers of Scottish and Baptist churches. Festivals of the various denominations take place throughout the year. Some sects such as the Dukhobors, Mennenites, Hutterites and Mormons are also represented. Missionaries have worked among the Indians since Louis XIII's day when Cardinal Richelieu supported the Jesuit Mission to the Hurons.

In 1931 Canada together with other British Dominions by a statute of Westminster was declared 'equal in status, in no way subordinate to each other.' From that time their common bond has been the British crown. The Queen's title is 'Elizabeth the Second, by the grace of God of the United Kingdom, Canada, and her other realms and territories, Queen, Head of the Commonwealth, Defender of the Faith.' She has no power but is a beloved symbol. She is represented by a Governor General whose official residence is in Ottawa and there are Lieutenant Governors in each province.

The prime minister and his cabinet actually govern. He is the leader of the party in power in Parliament. The cabinet appoints the members of the senate which is the Upper Chamber and ambassadors. The opposition, led by the head of the second largest party in the Commons, has twenty-five days of each parliamentary session to debate its priorities and on six of these days it can attempt to move a vote of no confidence. Should this succeed the prime minister must call new elections or resign. The Canadian flag, adopted as recently as 1965, has three vertical panels, the two outer being red and the centre one white with a red maple leaf superimposed.

In the cultural field Canada has produced fine writers and artists. Mazo de la Roche's saga of the Whiteoak family enjoys popularity equal to that of Galsworthy's Forsyte family. The adventures of the Whiteoaks continued in book after book and the reading public began to know each member intimately. Perhaps the favourite character was Grandmother Whiteoak who left Ireland to settle in Canada as a young married woman. When she was well over ninety she left the pages of the books briefly with her children and grandchildren and was put on the stage. Nancy Price acted her part superbly and the play had successful runs in both London and New York.

Long before the Whiteoaks had appeared on the scene the late Lucy Maud Montgomery of Prince Edward Island had created Anne of Green Gables in her famous book of that name. Although Anne only existed in the imagination of the authoress, she herself actually lived in a most attractive house called Green Gables. When she died the house became a museum and tourists refuse to believe that Anne, a little red-haired girl, is a myth. Hundreds of visitors tour the house each summer season. In a way Anne does live because the favourite musical on Prince Edward Island is—you have guessed it—*Anne of Green Gables.*

Stephen Leacock is perhaps one of the best known humourists in the English-speaking world and his *Nonsense* novels are now classics. Another successful writer who excels in depicting the Canadian way of life is Hugh Maclennan. In his book *Barometer Rising,* he describes the true story of two ships, one carrying munitions, colliding in Halifax harbour during the First World War. It has often been referred to as 'the largest man-made blast prior to the atom bomb', and it destroyed half the city. Hugh Maclennan writes about it so brilliantly that you feel you can see the holocaust. One of the most famous poems to result from the same period was written by Doctor John McCrae—'In Flanders Fields'.

Of the painters there are of course the well known Group of Seven, the first artists to use Canadian landscapes, especially winter scenes, as subjects. Inspired by a sensitive artist-backwoodsman, Tom Thomson (1877-1917) they, as one of the founder members H. Y. Jackson wrote, 'treated our subjects with the freedom of the decorative designer. We tried to emphasise colour, line and pattern'. However, 'a prophet is not without honour save in his own country', and their work went largely unnoticed until they were 'discovered' at the Wembley exhibition in 1923. They were further acclaimed at the Paris Exhibition of 1927. Hennessey and Coborne composed winter farming scenes, Jackson did the same, his farm buildings and fences half submerged in snow, stark hills in the background. Gagnon depicted the old habitant way of life in northern Quebec.

Later Emily Carr painted Indian scenes with totem poles, hawk-faced braves and the soft gloom of forests.

When it comes to drama the Festival Theatre at Stratford, Ontario, is perhaps the best known internationally but there are other theatres throughout the country which offer a very high standard. The Royal Winnipeg Ballet and the National Ballet of Canada also enjoy a great reputation. In medicine Dr Frederick Banting and Charles Best were the discoverers of insulin and in 1876 Alexander Graham Bell produced the first successful outdoor telephone transmission. Lester Pearson won the Nobel Peace Prize and then there are the great paper barons like Lord Beaverbrook and Lord Thomson; and so one could go on....

For those who enjoy boating and hunting there is ample opportunity right across the country, and for ski enthusiasts many resorts. In recent years as well as ordinary skiing, cross country has become popular, snowshoeing and tobogganing are also having a revival. Rented equipment is available at most sports centres. Snowmobiling is a fairly new sport and is expanding rapidly. Ice hockey and skating are familiar to most youngsters. One of the most famous places to watch really fast skating is on the Rideau Canal in Ottawa. It is one end of the waterway that links with Kingston. It is just behind the Parliament buildings and among the masses of skaters do not be surprised to see politicians and businessmen on their way to meetings swinging their brief cases from side to side.

The new enormous underground plazas and shopping centres are intriguing, especially those in Toronto and Montreal where there are almost complete towns beneath the city centres. You can shop in air-conditioned comfort and walk where you please no matter how much traffic there is or how inclement the weather above. There are shops of all kinds, restaurants and banks. Canadian souvenirs are many and varied. The handicrafts made by the Indians, Eskimos, and French Canadians include carvings, hooked rugs, paintings, jewellery, leatherwork and pottery. Beautiful ship models can be bought in the Maritimes.

Now that the amount of air luggage is regulated by dimension rather than weight it is possible to take with you one or two useful extras. Some fairly stout walking shoes will be helpful for sightseeing in the national and provincial parks. There you will get plenty of opportunity to use the camera and binoculars which you can carry as personal luggage. Black bears, coyotes, moose and other animals wander freely and frequently cross the roads.

2 GATEWAY TO THE PACIFIC AND WESTERN CANADA— BRITISH COLUMBIA

It takes nine-and-a-half hours to fly from Heathrow to Vancouver on the daily Air Canada jumbo service. We touched down smoothly at British Columbia's main air terminal on Sea Island south of the city, one hot September day. It was hard to believe that our non-stop journey, cocooned in comfort, had carried us over the inhospitable Arctic wastes while we were served meals, watched a movie and listened to music. The bus ride of some 7½ miles (12 kilometres) left no doubt about Vancouver's claim to be one of the most beautiful cities in North America. This was further emphasized when our bus decanted us at the Sheraton Landmark and we could gaze out over it from our room on the thirty fifth floor.

As I looked down over one of the busiest ports in the Pacific, I wandered back in my mind to my childhood spent in a port on the diametrically opposite side of the continent—St John's, Newfoundland. The blue water was scattered with boats of all kinds, gleaming passenger ships, yachts, barges, fishing boats and rafts of timber on tow. Vancouver city, built on a peninsula, is only 44 square miles (114 square kilometres) and we were in the 'downtown' section. To right and left of us were hotels, banks and other highrise buildings intersected by avenues where brightly coloured cars sped, small as children's toys, stopping now and then at traffic lights. A yellow sea-bus ferry made its dignified departure across Burrard Inlet, no doubt carrying commuters to 'greater' Vancouver. A float-plane made a dash along the water and then took off perhaps for Victoria, perhaps carrying sportsmen to a favourite fishing lake. Another float-plane did the same thing, miraculously finding enough space to do so. Mountains edged into the horizon and black clouds suddenly swept up from behind them covering the sun with a sudden rainstorm. Half of the sky was dark, the rest still clear blue and gradually a brilliantly coloured rainbow knitted the two together.

There is so much to see in this port city that it is difficult to know where to begin. The parks and gardens with their luxuriant sub-tropical flowers and trees attract many people, the shops are inviting, the avenues wide, yet there are intimate areas such as Chinatown and Gastown. It is a completely individual city except for one thing: the Lions Gate Bridge, which spans the entrance to the harbour, does remind one of San Francisco's Golden Gate—and is just as beautiful.

You can go sightseeing in one of a fleet of British-type double-decker buses. These allow as much time as you would like at each place with a bus returning every hour. They also call at the main hotels. Chinatown and Gastown are interesting sections in the oldest part of Vancouver and both are places in which to meander. Gastown has four main streets criss-crossing each other, Water, Carrall, Cordova and Powell Streets. This quarter formed part of the original Vancouver as a sort of shanty town and was named after a notorious saloon keeper called Gassy Jack Deighton, although it is said that it was a 'dry' community until he came. There is a statue of this worthy sporting a large bow tie and standing on a keg in Maple Tree Square.

Quite recently the property developers wanted to raze the old buildings to the ground and replace them with modern ones but a revolt against this move defeated it and much of what can be seen today was done by students and volunteers. Street lights were replaced by Mock Victorian gaslights, the shabby warehouses were gutted, rebuilt and faced with red brick and you walk over the cobblestones to reach Maple Tree Square. Behind the pleasing red-brick façades are an array of restaurants and boutiques.

Of the Victorian-type restaurants with their wax-moustached waiters, the Old Spaghetti Factory, some 50 yards (45 metres) from Maple Tree Square, is amusing to say the least. Inside it has an old tram car which was built by the Columbian Railway Company in 1910. It has been fixed up as an intimate dining room within the restaurant. It used to run between Main and Cambie Streets until about twenty years ago when it just remained in the open until it was refurbished and placed in the Spaghetti Factory. The menu is entertaining and, as well as drawings of some of the Victoriana which have been placed among the aspidistras, it describes their 'Chicken à Factoria' as—'Chicken, the oldest of the domestic fowls, was regarded by the Romans as sacred and by the Greeks as a gift from the gods, honour which did not, however, save the birds from being eaten—with our spaghetti.' Above the

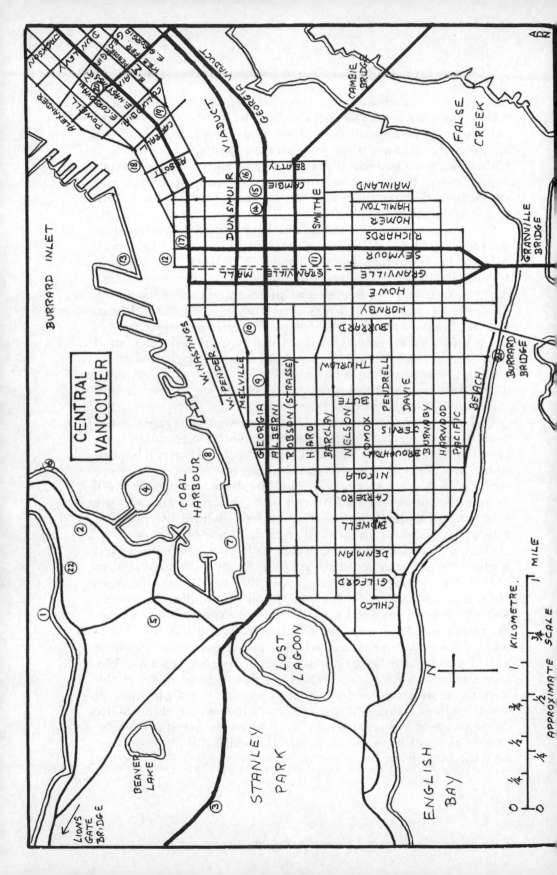

price lists are the words, 'Sorry, due to the extremely low prices we must charge a minimum of $2.25 per person.'

The clockwork mechanism of Gastown's slender Steam Clock at the corner of Cambie and Water Streets was made by Gill and Johnston, Croydon, England. The movement is a copy of an 1875 design. The clock sounds the hour and the Westminster chimes every quarter hour but instead of ringing bells the steam-driven clockwork mechanism activates steam whistles, the largest of which once announced the presence of a paddle steamer. The steam power is provided from an underground central heating main. It really is an amazing clock built and designed by Ray Saunders who says, 'The world's first steam clock has been created for the enjoyment of everyone,' and indeed this is so. It has four dials which are decorated with enamelled copper dogwood flowers—a greenish white blossom that appears in spring on the Pacific dogwood tree and is British Columbia's emblem. The dials are surrounded by a 24-carat gold-plated frame.

In a shop yard near the steam clock we watched an Indian carving a totem pole which lay on the ground. I went into the shop and enquired where it was going to be erected and was told it was a special order and was being shipped to Holland for someone's garden the following month. We asked if we might talk for a few minutes to the Indian who was carving it and we were led out to the yard through a side door. He was a young man and his wife and small daughter were watching him work. The totem pole was covered with drawings and the artist was carefully chipping away with an adze to define an eagle's beak. My husband asked how long it took

VANCOUVER

Key to map

1	Girl in Wet Suit	13	Sea Bus Terminal
2	Totem Poles	14	Post Office
3	Transcanada Highway	15	Queen Elizabeth Theatre and Playhouse
4	HMCS Discovery		
5	Zoo	16	Bus Terminal
6	Nine o'Clock Gun	17	Harbour Centre Observation Tower
7	Harbour Ferries Terminal		
8	Air West Seaplane Terminal	18	Gastown
9	Art Gallery	19	Chinatown
10	Visitors Information Centre	20	Police Station
11	Orpheum Theatre	21	Aquatic Centre
12	CPR Station	22	Cricket Pitch

to carve a totem pole. 'Don't know,' came the laconic reply, 'I've never done one before!'

Should you visit Gastown in late September you may be fortunate enough to strike two days of entertainment which take place each autumn. Needless to say it is held in honour of Gassy Jack Deighton. Pavement cafés appear outside the restaurants and two stages are erected where local musicians perform from noon until midnight where the revelry drowns traffic noises and seeps from Gastown into nearby Chinatown. Chinatown lives up to its name with oriental-style architecture—even the telephone booths have pagoda-shaped roofs. Many cities and towns boast of having the largest or the smallest office building in the world but in Chinatown there is what is thought to be the thinnest office building. It is 5 feet 10 inches (1.78 metres) wide and is a mere two storeys high.

When Jacques Cartier first sighted Canada he thought he was in China since he was indeed searching for it, but although he soon discovered he had not landed in the Orient, many years later the Orient came to Canada. Today there are some 70,000 Chinese in Vancouver, the largest Chinese community, after San Francisco, in North America. Chinatown's restaurants and street markets are as enticing as those in Hong Kong and you can buy the same things, such as dragon jars, tiger balm, kites and, unexpectedly, jade.

Two years ago in England I was given a jade brooch by an Egyptian friend. It was in the form of a spray of emerald-green bamboo leaves. I asked if it had been bought in an antique shop. 'No,' said my friend, 'I was on a convention in Vancouver and bought it in the shop at the hotel where I was staying. They make the most lovely jade jewellery there. Didn't you know jade was indigenous to British Columbia?' No, I did not—but I do now and it is a fascinating story.

Jade artifacts were found in Indian graves and in the 1800s boulders of jade were discovered in the Fraser river valley but caused little interest to men seeking gold. Later a Lieutenant Storey rediscovered the boulders and was interested enough in what the Chinese call the 'quintessence of heaven and earth' to explore further. He went on to find actual jade mountains some 150 miles (240 kilometres) north of the river's source. How the jade is quarried and who fashions the lovely pieces I have not yet discovered but exquisite things can be bought in the Vancouver shops both in Chinatown and elsewhere.

Granville Mall is a fashionable pedestrian shopping quarter

having many well-known stores. Then there is Robsonstrasse, so called because of its European-style shops, some complete with tinkling bell as you open the door. You can buy delicious fare for picnics in the delicatessen, cheese and pastry shops. There are many restaurants along this street where the numbers on the buildings reach into the thousands. They cater for individual palates, Swiss, German and, of course, Chinese. The French L'Eglantier has some tasty dishes, veal kidney with creamed mushroom and red wine sauce, tenderloin tips of beef cooked and wrapped in a pancake, fresh scallops with garlic, lemon and parsley. Strangely enough for a French restaurant it remains open all afternoon and you can have fresh cream chestnut cake and other mouthwatering items served with a variety of teas, such as chrysanthemum and honey.

With the fabulous views over the city and the surrounding country it is *de rigueur* to dine in an observation deck atop one of the highrise buildings. Many Canadian cities have these restaurants, often rotating to enhance the outlook, but Vancouver offers a choice of two. At the Harbour Centre plaques tell you what you are seeing as you gyrate. Remember not to put your handbag on the window ledge unless you want to wait some time to get it back!

One evening at the Sheraton Landmark we had dinner on the forty-second floor in the Cloud 9 revolving restaurant and had 'The Royal Trio' for a main course—fillet mignon, Alaska crab and a lobster tail served with tiny carrots, a baked potato and green salad. It was as well we had skipped lunch that day. The lights were twinkling out over the water and high over Grouse Mountain.

Without question the biggest tourist attraction in Vancouver is the Grouse Mountain skyride only 15 to 20 minutes from the centre of the town. Cable cars carry passengers to and from the peak. At the top there is a restaurant modelled on a Swiss chalet, known as the Grouse Nest which fits perfectly into a belt of trees. Perched some 3,940 feet (1,200 metres) above Vancouver, you can have a meal and enjoy a view better than any artist could paint. It is really breathtaking. You gaze down at the city on its tongue of land merging into the sea, the tip being the lovely green Stanley Park—what look like tiny matchsticks are in fact totem poles. Beyond the tall buildings, sometimes peeping through the clouds, the water stretches blue as a sapphire, the Lions Gate Bridge is strung across the harbour entrance and the whole scene is banded by mountains.

The mountain air has the same effect on the tourist as a glass of vintage wine, slightly heady and invigorating and there is plenty to do and see. There are hang-gliding contests and demonstrations, a mono-rail coaster and special gift shops. From December to April the slopes are a challenge for skiers and the major runs are lit until 11.30 p.m., seven days a week. A snow-making system ensures good conditions if nature does not. In summer there is hiking and picnicking. You sometimes see mountain goats with curly horns on crags, but I got my biggest surprise when a great St Bernard dog came up to me wagging his tail and posed for a photograph. He was not Swiss and he did not have a small keg of brandy around his neck but his name reminded me of both—Brandy. Not to be missed at the Grouse Nest are the dinner and Sunday Brunch 'Flight Specials'.

The drive out of town to Grouse Mountain takes you through Stanley Park and over the Lions Gate Bridge spanning the harbour mouth. On a clear day as you cross the bridge you can see ahead of you the twin peaks resembling lions' heads which gives the bridge its name. You follow Capilano Road and shortly come to a small park on your left with a large gift shop at the entrance. Here you can buy a ticket to walk over the Capilano suspension foot bridge. It is about 490 feet (150 metres) long and is strung across the deep gorge of the Capilano River. Since 1899 it has been crossed and recrossed by thousands of people. The bridge is about 245 feet (75 metres) above the river and many visitors refuse to traverse its swaying narrow length. However, handrails give confidence and, although it swings from side to side as you gingerly cross it, the view from it and the sensation of being suspended in space by a few wires rather like hang gliding, are well worth any sensation of mild nausea at walking on something so insubstantial. Birds fly through tall Douglas firs far below, and down deeper the river snakes its way through mossy boulders. It is not advisable for those who fear heights to cross the bridge because, once over the canyon, you have to recross it to return to your car. Back near the gift shop called the Capilano Trading Post, you can browse among native handicrafts such as hand-made jewellery and small, carved totem poles. If you have your camera there are several wooden totem poles and life-size Indian statues carved from red cedar wood in the park, not to mention a wigwam, for the Capilano River is still one of the Indian fishing grounds and they live nearby. There is also a salmon hatchery and not far away Cleveland Dam, which provides much of Vancouver's drinking water.

The city has several important museums and the planetarium, with its conical roof, has a curious surrealistic sculpture in front of it. It is over 20 feet (6 metres) high and, with its many steel tentacles, looks rather like a giant crab. The illusion is further emphasized by a fountain over it.

Off Marine Drive you will find the extensive grounds, 1,000 acres (405 hectares), of British Columbia University. The campus boasts Japanese gardens, a fine arts gallery and a totem pole park. Of the other parks, the Queen Elizabeth is prettiest with sunken garden, arboretum and a fabulous rose garden. Being on the highest elevation in the city it has lovely views in all directions.

One of the best-known features of Vancouver surely must be Stanley Park. Only five minutes' drive from the busy city centre and situated at the end of the thumb of land on which Vancouver stands, it seems to have everything. It is rimmed by the sea on three sides and covers 1,000 acres (405 hectares). The lavish hand of nature has been preserved and augmented and 50 miles (80 kilometres) of scenic paths and tracks have been laid out. There are some 100,000 trees in the woods many of them Douglas fir and giant red cedars. Vancouver's 9.00 p.m. gun echoes from the park every evening.

A 7 mile (11 kilometre) promenade edging the sea offers several interesting places to stop. There is a lighthouse, a figurehead from an early sailing ship and then suddenly one day when I was sauntering by I felt I must be in Copenhagen. There on a rock just off shore perched the little mermaid. But no, it is Vancouver's slightly more reticent version, the Girl in the Wet Suit.

There is something for everybody in Stanley Park, a miniature train and zoo for the youngsters, tennis courts, bowling greens, miniature golf, cycling and even cricket for the sports enthusiasts. Of course there is a zoo for the grown-ups too and an aquarium which has dolphins and killer whales performing several times a day. There are picnic grounds, snack bars, a restaurant, swimming beaches and pools, quiet groves and flower gardens. Everybody goes there, locals and visitors alike, yet there is room for people to spread out unless you go to a concert or gather together for one of the annual festivals such as the Vancouver Folk Music Festival which goes on for three days in August. The most enjoyable festival of all takes place on the three evenings before Christmas. A flotilla of small ships, dressed overall with Christmas lights and with choristers in the leading ship, circumnavigates the harbour passing close to the shore of Stanley Park. The carols float across

the water and everyone joins in the singing—a fitting end to each
year.

A lasting memory was driving in the park with a friend who
stopped to let a string of Canada geese cross the road. Apparently
this is quite a common event and later I was shown a picture of
other cars doing the same thing. The caption read 'Honkers meet
Honkers'.

Ferries link Vancouver Island and the mainland carrying all
classes of vehicles including buses to and from various destinations.
Additionally, four small air lines, some using seaplanes which land
in the harbour close to the city centre, provide frequent services
for the visitor. Certainly there is no feeling of being cut off. Victoria
nestles on the southern tip enjoying plenty of sunshine, cool nights
and a welcome lack of humidity. Vancouver Island is often referred
to as Canada's Four Seasons' Island of the Pacific and is some 280
miles (450 kilometres) long and 93 miles (150 kilometres) wide.
The island's west coast is quite wild whereas the east coast is built
up. Highway 4 takes you to Long Beach and the lovely Pacific
Rim Park. There are mountains, streams, hiking trails and camping
sites. The ferries land at Nanaimo, the second largest town and
from there it is some 68 miles (110 kilometres) to Victoria.

Two hundred years ago, the famous explorer and navigator
Captain James Cook RN sailed his two ships, 'Resolution' and
'Discovery', along the coast of British Columbia in search of the
northern sea passage between the Pacific and Atlantic oceans. He
anchored in Nootka Sound on Vancouver Island to refit and repair
his ships. He was not to know that one day Victoria, the Canadian
city furthest from Britain, would turn out to be the most English
with stately homes and historic buildings. Double-decker buses
amble through squares where fountains cascade in the sunshine.
They pass the Royal London Wax Museum where, as in Madame
Tussaud's, richly costumed historic scenes bring kings and queens
back from the past. Life-size figures of such famous people as Elvis
Presley and Bob Hope look as if they will shake your hand, while
mythical figures from 'Star Wars' welcome you aboard their
spacecraft.

The nearby Parliament Building, erected in 1897, brings you
back to earth—yet not entirely. At night the whole building with
its dome is outline by thousands of golden lights giving it the
aspect of a dream palace floating in the air and reflected in the
inner harbour. Opposite the Parliament Building the famous ivy-
covered Empress Hotel stands like a proud Duchess. English tea

is a 'must' and it is said that more affairs of state are discussed there over the English muffins than in the distinguished building opposite. But perhaps the most English feature of all is the hanging flower baskets, on the lamp posts. Since 1937, when Victoria celebrated her seventy-fifth anniversary, they have become an institution—and what a delightful one. Through the summer months from June until the end of September nearly one thousand baskets provide a riot of colour.

Everyone imagines that the watering of the flowers must be the greatest headache but in fact this is the easiest of problems and is accomplished by one man. He operates a right-hand drive truck equipped with a 500 gallon (2,273 litre) water tank and applies water through an aluminium pipe shaped like a shepherd's crook with a spray nozzle on the end. As the work is done between 11.00 p.m. and 7.30 a.m. the flowers are happy because they have all night to drink and, during the day, passers-by can admire their beauty. Seeds are started in greenhouses, trailing lobelia having the first sowing and eventually the plants are inserted in their baskets and hung in place.

The island has green grass and flowers throughout the year and gets some 140 hours more sunshine during an average summer than the mainland opposite, due to a warm Pacific current. During this time Victoria Harbour is choc-o-bloc with visiting yachts and motor boats basking in the fine weather. Horsedrawn wagons for the tourists, shopping malls, colourfully dressed people, the sails of the yachts and the float planes all provide a chiaroscuro before a backdrop of totem poles in Thunderbird Park.

The Indians used to cut the branches off the tall cedar trees and carve their straight trunks with motifs to show other tribes how their history emerged and their relationship to their own magnificent animal, bird and fish friends. Some of the tribesmen had the fleetness of the deer, the fine sight of the eagle, their maidens the beauty and purity of mother-of-pearl. So the Indian grafted his history onto the tall trunks of giant cedars—their own version of the family tree.

The Oak Bay Beach Hotel is part of the life of Victoria, and has an intriguing secret life as well as a public one. Here for over fifty years famous people have come and gone without anyone being the wiser—crown heads from Europe and the Far East, millionaires, industrialists and ambassadors. Two guest books are kept, one with real names for the manager, the other with fictitious ones for the staff and general public. This can give rise to amusing situations.

For instance when Andy Williams the famous TV and singing star was there recently he heard someone say, 'Gosh, that chap looks the double of Andy Williams.' Of course sometimes the famous, or infamous, have made it their business not only to stay at the Oak Bay Beach Hotel but to be *seen* to have stayed there! Be that as it may the hotel itself is full of atmosphere and beautiful things.

First of all there is 'The Snug'. This dates back to a custom still observed in some English pubs when patrons for some reason or other do not wish to be seen in a local bar. The barman needs to have some discretion. The Vicar might drop by for a glass of sherry with a friend, the local policeman might pop in for a pint or matters of state could be discussed.

Throughout the hotel there are many beautiful pieces of furniture, most of them brought from Europe, which will interest the connoisseur. In the main lobby you will see the 'Crusader's Chair'. It is carved with intriguing symbols of a Norman keep, a fish and rope motif and those most splendid of creatures—lions. The mail box at the reception desk is not only a priceless antique but the most beautiful I have ever seen. In the early days no food was served to transients. Guests stayed for weeks at a time and ceremony was the order of the day. Afternoon high tea was a social occasion. The original hotel was burned to the ground in October 1930 and immediately a new building arose on the ashes and traditions of the old.

The Oak Bay Beach Hotel has the sea right on its doorstep, and its English-style gardens reach down to its driftwood-strewn beach. Killer whales, seals, salmon and schools of fish of all kinds go past the backdoor and many seabirds winter in the bay. There is a resident colony of fat mallard ducks in the hotel grounds, and even a friendly neighbourhood sea serpent. Cadborosaurus, the monster of Cadboro Bay, like his friend Ogopogo on the mainland, is a product of Indian legend and mythology. An Indian boy attempted to woo a daughter of the gods, and as punishment was turned into a sea serpent and sentenced to swim in Cadboro Bay for one million years. There have been reputed sightings of the strange beast during the past fifty years.

Bill Wright, owner of Sealand Oceanarium which is about a mile from the Oak Bay Beach Hotel, called there one August morning and asked to see Bruce Walker the proprietor. He enquired if there was space for a VIP who was visiting Sealand. Bruce said he was sorry but the hotel was fully booked. When Bill replied that this did not matter because his guest would prefer sleeping at the end of the back garden near the beach, Bruce was astonished to say the least. At his look of surprise Bill told him the guest would be an unusual one, a baby killer whale—and a very sick one at that. Could it be put in the old unused salt water pool? This was agreed.

The baby whale had been separated from its family when it should have still been suckling its mother. It had a bullet wound behind the dorsal fin, two on the opposite side, net abrasions and propeller wounds. It was not known how the whale became separated from its pod (family) or who had injured her but somehow she had made her way into warm shallow waters and had made friends with a sport fisherman, Bill Davis. Bill fished regularly in Menzies Bay and, realizing that the whale was too young to feed herself, fed her a few pounds of herring each day. When the whale allowed him to touch her he saw that she was very sick indeed and sent for help. You will be able to read the whole fascinating story in a book written by Paul Jeune. Suffice to say here that she was nursed back to health by an untiring rescue team. Although at times it was believed she would not survive, miraculously she did and so was given the very suitable name of 'Miracle'.

As she put on weight and regained her health it was decided to lift her by helicopter to a much larger pool at Sealand. A padded plastic sling was constructed and slipped round Miracle's sides and she was gently borne aloft and made a spectacular trip through the air. She thrives in her new quarters, learns quickly and can perform any trick which she is shown almost at once.

Despite the fact that Miracle is so clever and quite the largest draw at Sealand, she will never know that she is recorded as the Oak Bay Beach Hotel's longest staying guest, having enjoyed the luxury of the outdoor salt water pool for more than six months. She also holds the record for receiving outside guests during her stay. Wire fencing had to be erected overnight to keep back the crowds, for some 3,000 visitors came to see her most days. She may not have appreciated all this but she thoroughly enjoyed the salmon and other delectable fish sent to her by admirers and friends.

Besides the Sealand Dolphinarium, Victoria has amazing undersea gardens at Oak Bay Marina which over 4,000,000 people have visited. You descend a sloping staircase into an 'underwater' theatre and look through windows at the marine life around you. All kinds of fish lurk in their natural habitat—salmon, wolfeels, octopuses and seals. Considering the underwater traffic problems it seems amazing that nothing bumps into anything else—not even the scuba divers!

Twelve miles (19 kilometres) from Victoria are the Butchart Gardens, the happy inspiration of Mrs Jennie Butchart, whose husband Robert was a pioneer in cement manufacturing in Canada. Mrs Butchart decided to accept the challenge of beautifying the quarried area that formed part of their estate overlooking Tod Inlet. Starting in 1904 with a few scattered sweet peas and some roses, she began to create one of North America's most magnificent gardens. Through the years hundreds of tons of soil were carted into the barren area and thousands of shrubs and native flora planted to help hide the ugly scars. During their world travels the Butcharts collected unusual statuary, new rare plants, seeds and exotic shrubs which were gradually absorbed into a colourful series of formal gardens linked by paths, bridges and walkways. The Butcharts named their gardens 'Benvenuto', the Italian for 'Welcome' and opened them to the public.

In 1964, to commemorate their sixtieth anniversary, a fountain was added which is a masterpiece of the interplay of colour and water, even more so by night. As the gardens are so well known and attract many visitors, this in turn provides the money for continuous improvement and alteration. As well as the obvious attraction to the expert of so many exotic varieties of flora, floodlighting for evening openings, the expert blending of colour and the careful use of perspective in layout make a visit for the merest garden tyro a vivid experience.

Then there are the Fable Cottage Estate and the Olde England Inn to visit. The first was made by a married couple who decided to build a sort of Hansel and Gretel cottage and to actually live in it—a cottage just for two people. Room leads into room with low crooked ceilings, hidden nooks down to the floor, fireplaces, built-in window seats overlooking flower beds, rockeries and the seashore. News of this fairytale cottage spread and it became such an attraction that, almost before the couple moved in, so many people came to see it that they had to move out again; but not before they had constructed half life-size animated dwarfs doing all kinds of carpentry from sawing wood to making door hinges in the garden. Apart from the long lines of grown-ups who come to view Fable Cottage it is a lovely place to take children.

The Olde England Inn is an hotel where the words of James Boswell ring true—'There is nothing which has yet been contrived by Man which provides more happiness than a good inn.' Built in 1946 Olde England Inn is named after the original one situated on the shores of Lake Windermere in England's Lake District. Designed by a Yorkshireman, T. M. Slater, one of Victoria's finest architects, it was built by British craftsmen who were brought out to construct many of the fine houses in Victoria. It looks like an old seventeenth-century Tudor mansion and the entrance is through a panelled and beamed baronial hall. The atmosphere is further enhanced by the grounds where a whole English village has been laid out including exact copies of famous old buildings in England such as Dickens' Old Curiosity Shop and Anne Hathaway's cottage. The lovely old-world garden has crazy paving and herb beds. Many of the flowers and trees which grow are mentioned in Shakespeare's plays and the seeds were obtained from Stratford on Avon. The meals served at Olde England Inn are in the Henry VIIIth tradition including that wonderful roast of Tudor times—Baron of Beef.

Victoria is full of surprises and yet familiar. Over half a century ago Rudyard Kipling described it thus: 'To realize Victoria you must take all that the eye admires most in Bournemouth, Torquay the Isle of Wight, the Happy Valley at Hong Kong, the Doon, Sorrento and Camps Bay; add reminiscences of the Thousand Islands and arrange the whole round the Bay of Naples, with the Himalayas for background.'

Returning from Victoria to the mainland there are several places in British Columbia which are of interest to the visitor. The area around Hope has many resorts. The reason for the name is a curious one. Some years ago half a mountainside rolled slowly down the roadway. Fortunately no one was killed in its path and it only removed part of the surface and a tract of forest, so the district was named Hope. You can actually see where the mountain slid down and what happened. It is an unusual phenomena but rather spoiled because so many people have scrawled their names over the large boulders and rocks.

Even more impressive than Hope is the Hell's Gate gorge on the Fraser River near Lytton. A sinister, frightening canyon only 115 feet (35 metres) wide at the bottom where as much as 200 million gallons (909 million litres) of turbulent water surge through every minute. You can descend in a Swiss-made aerial tramway to watch the thundering water and actually browse through a gift shop at the bottom. Where Indians used to drive pegs into the rockface to get through the canyon in olden days, you can now watch trains snaking their way through tunnels. Most interesting as well is a vast fish ladder which enables some 200 million salmon to leap up each year on their way to their spawning grounds.

In complete contrast to the wildness of Hell's Gate are the fruit-growing area around Penticton and the vineyards of the Okanagan Valley. You can visit the Casabello winery in Penticton from 10.30 a.m. to 4 p.m. and sample some of the company's wines. Casabello makes champagnes, sherries and ports as well as red and white dinner wines. The pinot noir grape thrives in this district and climate.

3 GATEWAY TO THE NORTH — ALBERTA

Edmonton, capital of Alberta, is strategically placed right in the centre of the province. A mere century ago it was a fur-trading post on the banks of the north Saskatchewan river, later the last civilized spot on the way to seeking gold in the Yukon. Today it is the northernmost city of its size in North America. Between it and the Arctic lie vast tracts of spectacular wilderness.

Modern buildings reach for the sky in downtown Edmonton and form an uneven curtain wall along the river. Further away green pyramids also jut into the sky. This is nothing to do with Giza in Egypt, indeed there are not three pyramids but five. They are part of the Muttart Conservatory, a controlled environment growing area unlike anything else in Canada. The small central pyramid is a reception foyer while each of the others contains the flora of a specific zone. Tropical, arid and temperate displays are permanent features in three of the structures and the fourth is a showcase whose contents are changed now and then. These huge pyramids are not really green and are made of glass but the greenery inside gives the illusion in the distance. The Muttart is open daily and it is not only interesting to see the plants and trees but to notice how you feel physically in the different climatic conditions and to decide which suits you best.

Overlooking the river on the actual site of the original Fort Edmonton, stands the most familiar landmark in the city—the domed Legislative Building. It is designed in the form of a cross and its melodious carillon can be heard at midday and on Sunday afternoon. Its formal gardens are perhaps the most beautiful in the city. Adding to their attractiveness is the brightly burning centennial flame which was lit in 1967. On one side, flowers form a large maple leaf while on the other is the flower motif of Alberta—the wild rose. Also to celebrate 1967 as centennial year an ultra-modern museum was built which is unique. You walk along wide corridors passing scenes from the past up to the present. Life-size models are arranged as if on stage sets. Each background is hand-painted whether it represents outdoors or inside a building and the foregrounds are as realistic as the figures themselves. As you walk along and become engrossed in what you see, you would not be surprised to hear the fur traders and Indians bargaining, or see an animal walk towards you out of a forest or indeed watch a beaver swim across a lake. This feeling of being part of what you see is again apparent in Fort Edmonton Park where about 200 acres (80 hectares) will be developed eventually as a life-size diorama showing Edmonton's past. Already it includes an authentic reconstruction of the early trading post from which the city grew.

You can step back into the past literally during the latter part of July for some ten days when Edmonton honours those men and women who rushed off to the goldfields of the Yukon. The name of the festival is Klondike Days. People wear clothes of the gay nineties, shops don false façades with fancy lettered signs, cocktail bars and lounges become saloons and everywhere old songs are sung around tinny pianos. Sometimes there is even the sign above the pianist as in those honky tonk days when guns were pulled for any imagined insult—'Please don't shoot the pianist, he's doing his best!' The Exhibition Grounds revert to the past as well with a rowdy casino, horsedrawn garries, and at Chilkoot Mountain (an artificial creation) two hundred people at a time can see what it is like to pan for imitation gold. The tourists love Klondike Days as much as the locals and come prepared to act the part. Hourglass waists and plunging necklines are *de rigueur* and long dresses sweep over the grass. The men wear top hats and frock coats and crowd to the river to watch the exciting Sourdough River raft race, the ladies being careful not to get their period dresses splashed.

Children love 'Valley Zoo' akin to Disneyland, where small animals and birds are housed in Mother Goose settings. As soon as the children enter the fairy castle gates they are in nursery rhyme world with such well known people and animals as Humpty Dumpty, Goldilocks and the Three Bears, the Three Little Pigs and Mary's Little Lamb. If they get tired walking around there is a miniature railway.

The Queen Elizabeth Planetarium was the first to be built in Canada but now it has an even more pleasing boast—it is the smallest. Restaurants cater for every taste from gourmet meals at such places as Canadian Pacific's Chateau Lacombe, with its revolving rooftop dining room, to snack bars. Middle price places such as steak houses and Chinese restaurants abound. If you are a health food addict and pine for fresh salads and warm bread straight from the oven such places are easy to find. Just to mention one, there is The Palms at 102nd street just off Jasper Avenue. Here you can choose what is called a 'Creative Sandwich'. The owner waits as you decide what you would like to mix on an open sandwich from a long shelf of delicious vegetables and fruit — rather Scandinavian.

Edmonton has something for everyone, although the population is less than half a million, for the very good reason that it is fantastically rich — oil rich. The famous Leduc Oilfields were discovered in 1947 and shortly afterwards more petroleum was found at Red Water and Woodbend. These three fields form a girdle around Edmonton. It was as though the Klondike gold days had returned.

During the seventies international business interests focused on Edmonton. In 1978 the Commonwealth Games drew thousands of sport-lovers there. The city has little unemployment, no sales tax and it can afford to be one of Canada's foremost spenders on education and health.

Despite the highrise office buildings, super hotels and an ultra-modern network of pedestrian pavements (called 'pedways') connecting shopping malls and restaurants underground, Edmonton still retains much of its old-world charm. The Lieutenant Governor was a Cree Indian during 1979 and when he and his wife had their fiftieth wedding anniversary they refused to have any fuss and went back to their tribe for a simple celebration. In memory of the pioneers of the original big oil strike, the monument chosen was not a great concrete creation but the first oil derrick to find the precious liquid. It was brought from Leduc oilfield and set up as a lasting reminder at the southern entrance of the city.

The two booming oil cities of Edmonton and Calgary, some 180 miles (290 kilometres) apart, feud somewhat like the Hatfields and McCoys in the old western song. Not that the two towns pull guns or even draw swords, but they certainly squabble amicably and sharpen their wits at each other's expense. 'Why,' writes a Calgarian, 'doesn't Edmonton just put up a booth at the Calgary Stampede and forget about trying to do something on its own?' It is true that Edmonton is envious of Calgary's world-famous annual Stampede but at the same time Calgary, which is the oldest city in Alberta, is not too pleased that Edmonton was chosen as provincial capital! Be that as it may, they have a lot in common. Edmonton has Fort Edmonton Park and Calgary her Heritage Park, both have planetariums and spend oodles of money on ultra-modern museums. So it goes on but perhaps the greatest thing they share in common is the blessed chinook.

The chinook is a prevailing westerly wind originating in the Pacific. Crossing British Columbia it loses most of its moisture. Continuing over the Rockies it spreads out over Alberta plains bringing pleasant warmth and counteracting the freezing prairie weather during the coldest months of the year. Sometimes when the chinook is really strong, winter can only thrive for a few short weeks.

To the visitor at first glance Calgary seems a typical modern city but it differs in two respects which give it individuality. Some time in 1875 it began as a Mounted Police and trading post. The city was created by the coming of the Canadian Pacific Railway. In 1886 a great fire reduced the town to ashes in a few hours. When Calgary was reborn a sensible law was passed to forestall a repetition. The local attractive sandstone was to be used in future for building in place of timber. This is why Calgary is sometimes referred to as 'Sandstone City'. The other special feature is that it has a magnificent setting. It lies like a cup in a vast saucer, with to one side the confluence of the spectacular Bow and Elbow rivers, and the remainder encircled by green prairie and the gradually rising foothills of the Rockies.

Calgary enjoys great wealth which is still increasing. At the beginning of the century gold was found, cattle ranching has been big business for many years—it is probably the largest 'meat' city after Chicago—and now the ranch lands are proving to have enormous oil deposits beneath them. No small wonder the brochures call her 'the rugged, the restful, the spirited and the cosmopolitan'.

As the Calgary Stampede takes place in early July and Edmonton Klondike Days the latter part of the same month, you can take in both these festivals on a single trip. As the actual dates change from year to year it is advisable to find out the details before making your arrangements. One drawback about the Stampede is that it is booked so long ahead that it is difficult to find hotel or motel accommodation. Also, over this period, costs escalate to whatever the trade will bear and, if you are not staying with friends or relatives, it is wise not only to book well ahead but to check on prices.

Stampede Park is used for ordinary horse racing during the summer but, when the ten-day festival is in full swing, the rodeo atmosphere takes over. Ranchers, cowboys, Indians and visitors all converge on the town and, if businessmen go to their offices, they do so clad in their stetsons and string ties. Local people and tourists meet over street corner breakfasts of coffee and flapjacks. Even the red-coated Mounties join in the fun.

The Stampede events are rousing, especially the daily chuckwagon races when horse teams pull covered wagons around the racetrack, urged on by frantically shouting cowhands. You can visit gambling casinos, watch rodeo, livestock exhibitions, steer wrestlings and ropings, cowboys on bucking broncos, and other boisterous events and at night fireworks add to the noisy fun.

When you visit Calgary Zoo you may be surprised to find the 120 ton, 36 feet (11 metre) high model of a dinosaur called affectionately Dinny. Creatures like Dinny roamed some 90 miles (145 kilometres) north-east of Calgary millions of years ago. In this 22,000 acre (8,900 hectare) miniature desert, dinosaur skeletons have recently been excavated. This area is called the Badlands and its eerie lunar landscape also has great mushroom-shaped rocks known as 'hoodoos'.

The Calgary Zoo is a large interesting one and, should you tire walking around, you can have snack or cup of coffee in the conservatory which is also an aviary. I found the live animals far more interesting than Dinny, especially the grizzly bears which, although they have the reputation of being ferocious, are known to avoid man's presence in the open unless they are provoked. As they are mostly active during the night and early morning you are unlikely to meet them as you might an ordinary bear. Unfortunately the plains grizzly is almost extinct. Before the white man came to Canada they roamed the plains and hunted bison. The few that survive in the Rockies hunt elk, moose, sheep and goats.

Heritage Park was created by rebuilding houses and stores brought from nearby old towns on a 60 acre (25 hectare) peninsula in the Glenmore Reservoir. Heritage represents an early western Canadian anonymous town with its own steam railroad, firehall, horsedrawn streetcar, and paddle steamer.

The sophisticated shopping centre in Calgary is in sharp contrast. All the well-known stores like Eatons are here, pedestrian pavements are set with trees, flowers and fountains and most surprising and delightful of all is the 24 acre (10 hectare) glassed-in Devonian Gardens. It is a novel form of city park and includes a hundred shops on different levels. No matter what the weather outside it has sub-tropical trees, flowering shrubs and a reflecting pool in summer which is turned into a skating rink in winter. More than

15,000 trees and plants are arranged on three levels, and an inner courtyard interconnected by several escalators and two circular glass-enclosed elevators. You can listen to a concert while enjoying your lunchtime sandwich, or you can eat in a gourmet restaurant and, as elsewhere in Alberta, there is no sales tax on anything if you buy in the shops.

Al Bailey, a slim, tall man dressed in discreet cowboy garb and wearing an impeccable white stetson, took us to a cattle auction. Nearly 200 million dollars' worth of business a year passes through the Calgary stockyards and there are auctions every weekday morning. We were led upstairs to a series of elevated duckboard walkways above open pens containing cattle of all sizes. In the centre we entered the auction hall which seemed like an old-time theatre. It was semi-circular, with seats in rising tiers and a fenced pit replacing the stage. This contained the entry and exit doors and the auctioneer's podium.

Everyone wore cowboy clothes and we ourselves felt conspicuous in our everyday clothes. I asked if the three ladders in the middle of the ring below were to enable the staff to enter. 'No,' said Al, 'that is how they leave if a steer gets frisky!' The first animal came in with a young cowboy swishing the air with a stick which caused the steer to cavort.

'Why on earth is he doing that?' I asked. Al looked surprised. 'Every potential buyer wants to know if the animal is perfect and he can't judge that if it does not jump around a bit.'

The bargaining began and sounded to us exactly like the tobacco auctions one has heard and seen on TV, an unintelligible sing song. As soon as a beast was sold it was ushered out of the exit door and in a few seconds an illuminated sign above the podium indicated a figure. This was the weight of the animal and I thought it interesting that, contrary to the European system of recording the weight before the sale, here the buyer only finds it out after purchase.

It takes just over a minute to soar upwards in a lift to the top of the Calgary Tower and step onto the observation terrace. In the Panorama Room you can have lunch or dinner while the restaurant revolves. Steaks are a speciality and are served—so the menu says and I have warned you—'with a view to please.' There is also the Sightseer's Snack Bar. If such heights make you dizzy you can recover when the lift decants you at ground level by drinking a beer, or something stronger, in the Tower Olde English Pub—a replica of a fifteenth-century ale house.

The view from the tower is truly magnificent on a clear day when you can see the Rockies—but this is as nothing compared with visiting them, and Lake Louise is only 113 miles (180 kilometres) distant from Calgary.

The sheer beauty and loveliness of Lake Louise is impossible to describe. No matter how bored you are with tourists clicking cameras at everything they see, you really must take a camera to Lake Louise for, however much of an amateur you think you are, you are bound to get a photograph you will always treasure. There is much argument about the ideal time of day and conditions of weather to obtain the best picture. Ringed by mountains, the highest being Victoria Glacier which is always snowcapped, the period of sunlight is abnormally short and the shadows deep. The lake can be shrouded in mist and is almost unearthly in moonlight. This debate is even more hotly contested by artists and, if you do not have a camera, the Chateau Lake Louise has a small shop where there are pictures galore painted at different times of day as well as in different seasons.

Just as with the Taj Mahal in India, Chateau Lake Louise is perfectly sited in this idyllic mountain setting. It is an hotel in the grand style yet it started as a small chalet in 1890, consisting of a veranda, a sitting room, a kitchen and a few bedrooms. During the summer of 1892, fortunately while no one was around, it burned to the ground. A much larger chalet was built next spring which could accommodate a dozen guests. In those days visitors were few, but news of the beauty spot was getting about and a few people would come and camp nearby and use the chalet to have meals. During the early 1900s visitors increased to such an extent that two half-timbered wings were added and large open fireplaces installed. A road was built from the station and horsedrawn carriages would convey guests to the chalet. The charge was 50 cents per guest and hand luggage, and 75 cents extra for trunks. It was nearly an hour's drive from the station as the going was steep and there were two wooden bridges and one iron one to cross.

By the beginning of the First World War the chalet had grown into a good sized hotel. After the war more travellers came and further extensions were added. In 1924 a fire once again destroyed the building and the Chateau Lake Louise we see today gradually came into being.

During the twenties a tramline was built from the station to the chateau. Guests could buy a 25 cent ticket from the station, the fare being the same for either 'closed' or 'open' trams. This caused a few complaints and inspired the following Robert Service type ballad:

> In the noonday heat and warmth of the sun
> Seems the only time the closed cars run,
> But when it's blowing a gale
> And looks like snow
> In the open car we're sure to go.
> The passengers come and they take their seat
> And the first thing they say is, "Where is the heat?"
> To which we reply in the friendliest way
> "How much do you want for the little you pay?"

At the end of one summer season a cheerful guide, nicknamed Glory, decided to make it something to remember by riding his horse through the main doors of the Chateau, round the ballroom, up to the rotunda and thence through the back tunnel to the beer parlour. After Glory's equestrian feat, revolving doors were installed which it was said were there to prevent horses mingling with the guests.

Of course on this planet nothing is ever quite perfect and the only flaw we could find was that all the bedroom windows giving onto the fabulous view are fitted with fly screens. Keen photographers have obviously gone to great lengths to remove them as there are notices asking you not to do so. Theoretically if you hold your camera close to the screen it does not affect the photograph but many people are not convinced.

At least there is no question about the temperature of the lake water. It is deep and glacial always. Unless you were a polar bear or an Eskimo you could not possibly swim in it. The idea may be enticing but, if you are a lotus eater and lulled by beauty as others at Lake Louise, you will not attempt it—besides there is the Chateau's heated bathing pool!

The waters in the lake are usually written up as being 'emerald' but again it is a point that people dispute. Obviously the lake reflects the different shades of the trees and the colouring in the surrounding mountains, the sunlight on the snow in winter and the grass in summer. In paintings it is depicted in all shades of green from emerald to jade. To me it seemed the cool turquoise of an ancient Egyptian scarab. It is part of Lake Louise's charm for each visitor to carry away his own recollection of it.

Banff, in the Rockies 35 miles (56 kilometres) from Lake Louise, first became famous for its hot springs which bubble out of the ground. Queen Victoria was so impressed by this phenonomon that she ordered ten square miles (25 square kilometres) to be 'set aside' so that future generations could 'take the waters'. The springs have not only cured many invalids but Queen Victoria's ten square miles sparked off the idea for a national park which today exceeds 2,560 square miles (6,630 square kilometres). They have also given their name to a hotel similar to that at Lake Louise — the Banff Springs Hotel. When you see it for the first time you will not only rub your eyes with disbelief but do it again, for it looks like a chateau transported from the Loire by some rival of William Randolph Hearst. However, it was not, it just grew that way over the years through various renovations.

In the town of Banff a short distance from the hotel, the therapeutic hot springs feed baths and a swimming pool. Only recently when reading the autobiography of Agatha Christie, I learned that she once suffered from neuritis. On a visit to Banff she swam in the pool and, at the end where the hot sulphur spring water gurgles out, let it play over her shoulders. At the end of four days her neuritis had disappeared.

There are many hotels and motels in and around the town for this is one of the prime skiing places in Canada. Buses can take you to most of these and skiing equipment can be hired. Mount Norquay on the edge of the town offers steep or nursery slopes. Sunshine Village further away claims the best powder snow in the Rockies averaging 400 inches (1,016 centimetres) a season. From the top of Lookout Mountain there is a 2½ mile (4 kilometre) run down and, for those who enjoy the increasingly-popular sport of cross-country skiing, there are miles of pine-edged trails. Lake Louise has more than 70 miles (110 kilometres) of them. Do not be misled by the names given to some of these trails and slopes. Thus Deadfall may frighten you off and Tranquillizer may encourage you to try it but the names are not necessarily descriptive. Cable cars, called 'gondolas' in Canada, whisk you up to the heights of the Rockies and you will enjoy breathtaking views, summer and winter, which will long remain in your mind's eye.

It was the CPR President, the far-seeing William Cornelius Van Horne, who chose the site for the Banff Springs Hotel. He rightly sensed that when his passengers disembarked for a few days' sojourn, nothing would delight them more than a Shangri La setting which would certainly produce much word-of-mouth advertising. Expense was to be no object and Van Horne prepared sketches. The architect chosen was already well known, Bruce Price, and like any member of his profession, a commission where money was not to be a limiting factor proved very attractive. Incidentally the writer of the standard American work on etiquette, Emily Post, was his daughter.

Banff Springs Hotel went through many traumatic experiences before emerging as we see it today approaching its centennial. As with many other world-famous hotels it has had its fires and disasters, plans have been changed, wings added and renovations carried out yet, like so many of its contemporaries elsewhere, it remains an entity. The old Mena House at the foot of the pyramids in Egypt has been altered so many times that today it is on thirty different levels. Yet it looks as if it grew out of the golden sands around it. Indeed when asked by a visitor where Cheops stayed while his Great Pyramid was being built, a guide replied, 'At Mena House, Sir.' Shepherd's in Cairo is another world-famous hotel which, over 100 years old, has survived four rebuildings, the last not even on the same site, yet today it retains its dignity and ambience.

So the Banff Springs Hotel can hold its head up in this proud coterie and offer a tradition of service and hospitality which fully maintains its reputation. It was completely rebuilt in 1928 yet retains its atmosphere of earlier years when Cornelius Van Horne would stride through the entrance to make sure that the guests were having a good time with every luxury to hand. Perhaps the greatest point in its favour is its magnificent position amid the grandeur of the Rockies. Van Horne is supposed to have coined the phrase, 'Since we can't export the scenery we'll have to import the tourists!'

Crowned heads, celebrities, politicians, the famous and infamous flocked to the Banff Springs Hotel before and between the two great World Wars. King George VI and Queen Elizabeth accompanied by the Canadian Prime Minister MacKenzie King stayed there in 1939. The Queen was enchanted with the local wild flowers. The King of Siam tried to tempt the maître d'hotel at that time, Oscar Wulliman, away from the hotel to return with him to his palace, but although the maître accompanied him to Victoria to wait on him there, when the King left Canada, Oscar returned to Banff.

Occasionally people were ill mannered. One man, who had had too much drink, went up to another guest and asked in a loud voice, 'Where's the lavatory?'

'Straight down the hall,' came the reply. 'Turn right and you will see a door with the notice "Gentlemen" above it. Do not be deterred by this, just go straight in.' Today you can find all the appurtenances of a modern hotel: boutiques, discothèque, saunas and an Olympic-size swimming pool.

Banff is linked to Jasper some 150 miles (240 kilometres) away by the Icefield Parkway. To the north Jasper national park covers some 4,200 square miles (10,880 square kilometres) and the two towns, which give their names to the parks, are where most of the tourists stay. Bears, not to mention deer, wander fearlessly in the woods and even on the golf courses. The former it is said have learned how to turn on the sprinklers in the summer to cool themselves in the same way that they can turn trash containers upside down in search of something tasty to eat. This is the reason that the containers are all put in wire cages.

Driving on the highway from Banff to Jasper is an extraordinary experience as you are cutting right through what is called the Columbia icefield. About a dozen of the Rockies' twenty-five highest peaks are solid ice and the vast Athabasca Glacier fed by the Columbia icefield is 600 to 1,000 feet (180-300 metres) thick. The rate of melt at the toe, which you can visit from the road and actually touch, is more than its flow so that it retreats at the rate of one foot (30 centimetres) annually. As it does so it deposits a pulverized rocky substance. Even on the hottest summer day the area is cool and you can go for a ride in an oversnow vehicle or even climb a short distance over the glistening white ice whose movement is imperceptible. You will be overwhelmed by the strange beauty and sheer size of this novel environment.

Unfortunately we did not visit Medicine Hat, or indeed many other places, but this is the traveller's lament in any country and is the reason he is drawn back to the same place again and again. The very name 'Medicine Hat' has always appealed to me and several reasons have been given for its origin. The most likely seems to be that the Blackfoot invaded the territory of the Cree and fighting took place on a river bank. The Cree tribe kept the Blackfoot at bay until their medicine man suddenly fled and in doing so lost his headdress. The Cree took this as a doubly bad omen and surrendered. The site of the battle was called 'Saamis', an Indian word meaning 'Medicine Man's Hat'—later to be shortened to Medicine Hat.

Rudyard Kipling visited Medicine Hat on a trans-Canadian visit after he won the Nobel Prize. He was most interested to find that the city had been built over a reservoir of natural gas and described it as a city 'with all hell for a basement'. Some years later it was decided to change the city's name and the townsfolk were divided over the issue. Those who wished it to remain remembered how Kipling had liked it and sent him a round robin letter asking what he thought. He sent a long reply giving very good reasons why it should remain as it was, saying in part, 'It has no duplicate in the world; it makes men ask questions...it has qualities of uniqueness, individuality, assertion and power.'

Glass blowing is a thriving business in Medicine Hat and it also claims that each July it has the oldest rodeo and exhibition in Alberta.

4 THE PRAIRIE PROVINCES — SASKATCHEWAN AND MANITOBA

Saskatchewan is dove-tailed between the two other prairie provinces of Alberta and Manitoba. Its capital, Regina, with a population of about 150,000, is the largest of its eleven cities. At one time Regina was called Wascana, an Indian word meaning 'pile of bones' because of its great mounds of buffalo bones piled up by generations of hunters. Princess Louise, the wife of the Governor General, suggested the name of Regina as a compliment to her mother Queen Victoria and this it became. The name suits it well. Regina has a certain dignity having been for some time prior to that the capital of the Northwest Territories and the headquarters of the Royal Canadian Mounted Police. Its parks are spacious. Wascana Centre Park, 2,000 acres (800 hectares) in extent, on the banks of a lake, is full of things to do and see. Among these are the boyhood home of Canada's thirteenth Prime Minister, John G. Diefenbaker, moved from its original site, the Museum of Natural History, art galleries and the Regina campus of Saskatchewan University whose archives house the early history of the city. Sports such as boating and swimming are there for the asking as well as barbeque and picnic areas.

Although the Mounties' headquarters are now moved to Ottawa, Regina is still their main training centre and tourists crowd to see the barracks and the Little Chapel on the Square. In 1883 it was a military mess hall but was later converted into a chapel. The stained-glass windows depict scenes from a Mountie's life. The font was presented in memory of a mountie who was killed in the Riel Rebellion. The flags to the right and left of the chapel once flew over the Fort Walsh.

The Military Museum has many interesting items. There is the uniform worn by Superintendent Walsh, the man with whom the Indian chief Sitting Bull negotiated when he fled from the United States into Canada with his tribe. You can see the cross carried by

Riel on his way to the gallows in 1885. Later in the day there is the Sunset Ceremony which the Mounties give every evening during the summer at Wascana Centre.

Although Regina is situated on prairie land it has many trees. The local people were encouraged to plant them — and vied with each other to do so. It is said that you can tell the oldest part of the city by the height of the trees. This is not to say that there are no skyscrapers and actually the highrise buildings, especially those in the commercial section, appear to be higher than in other places. This is an illusion because of the flat terrain and they can be seen from many miles away as you approach the city.

The second largest town in Saskatchewan (the name is a Cree Indian word meaning 'Swift flowing', first used to describe the river that knifes across the province) is Saskatoon which came into being for the strangest of reasons — abstinence from alcohol. Founded in 1883 by a temperence colony from Ontario, at the end of twenty years there were still only 113 people living there — perhaps there is a lesson in this! However, that was some time ago and today the city contains 130,000 uninhibited citizens.

One of the benefits of developing a city during the twentieth century is the availability of the new art of town planning. Saskatoon's avenues and streets are not only tree lined but wide. An attractive place with six slender bridges tying it together across the South Saskatchewan river, and because of this sometimes called 'City of Bridges', its buildings are well spread out. The Mendel Art Gallery is famous for its Eskimo sculpture and collections of paintings by Canadian artists including the Group of Seven.

As 'Medicine Hat' sounds an illogical name for a town, so does 'Moose Jaw'. Between the latter and Regina endless miles of plains stretch, seemingly to the very horizon, producing some of the world's finest wheat called Number One Hard. As for Moose Jaw's name, one probability for the reason is that an Indian was surprised and fascinated to see a white man at the river's edge mending his wagon with the jaw of a moose!

It seems festivals are always held in July in the prairie provinces. Regina has its Buffalo Days with parades, street dancing and rodeos in which the tourists join townsfolk in western costume. Barbeques are at midday and after sunset but watch your figure because the day's fun begins with pancake breakfasts. Saskatoon's festival also in July, called Pioneer Days has historical pageants, agriculture and livestock shows. Competitions include threshing and harness racing.

Perhaps one day the town of Whitewood will have a festival of the 1880s and nineties. That was a time when some adventurous French Comtes, their retinues and families, came to Canada. Crippled by taxation in France and not too sure of the new republicanism, they decided to make new fortunes yet to retain their old way of life. Although they did not succeed they were enterprising. They chose the Whitewood area and built their houses and a church in the name of St Hubert.

One of the strangest miracles in the hunting world is told of St Hubert who lived at the beginning of the eighth century in Aquitania, France. He spent his youth indulging in worldly pleasures and was passionately fond of the chase. One day a stag appeared before him with a luminous cross between its antlers. From that day he is said to have repented of his way of life and of killing deer indiscriminately. Hubert became patron saint of hunters and gamekeepers. So a type of conservation was born and the 'Order of St Hubert' gave hunting a nobler meaning. Thus at Whitewood the Comtes could stalk deer for the larder but hunting buffalo was another matter. They refused to adapt themselves to local conditions but carried on their foolhardy life with zest and enjoyment.

Comte de Jukilhac ran a sheep farm, Comte de Langle raised race horses, Baron de Brabant grew chicory and Comte de Seysells founded a cheese factory. The sheep were a failure, race horses were not in demand; chicory, even canned, was too sophisticated a taste for the other pioneers as was the cheese, a type of exotic Gruyère. Even the Comte de Beaulincourt who was an artist could not sell his paintings.

Although most of these French nobles were ill advised by well-meaning friends in France as to how to augment their fortunes across the Atlantic, they managed somehow to live in the grand manner indeed — as others did with more success in Quebec. Coaches and dogcarts held together despite rough trails and rutted roads, white gloves and long ball gowns appeared at dances. Log cabins gave way to larger houses and for a while elegance and grace flourished, but the time was not ripe and the expense too great, so, like an exotic flower it withered overnight. Many of these adventurers managed to adapt to the new life but the others returned home. Although the manor houses have long since gone, stories of those days are remembered and the little church of St Hubert remains.

Food, like oil, is in such short supply in so many places that the demand is never fully met. Saskatchewan with its endless miles of waving wheat would appear utopian to much of the third world if they ever saw it. The province has many nicknames such as 'Breadbasket of the World' and 'The Grain Province', and over half the population are engaged in farming. Stephen Leacock, the famous Canadian humourist put it succinctly when he wrote 'The Lord said "let there be wheat" and Saskatchewan was born!'

For tourists who enjoy the outdoors there are different types of canoe holidays which have proved so popular that you can choose from some fifty trips. They range in duration from a day to more than two weeks, some ending where they began and others going from point to point. Water covers one-eighth of the province so there are innumerable lakes and streams. Fishing is exceptionally good and there are over two hundred fly-in or drive-in fishing camps. Licences and guides are a necessity and your travel agent is the best person to give you details. There is also the Saskatchewan Vacations Association to contact if you wish to have a farm holiday.

Shortly after leaving Whitewood you cross over the border into Manitoba. This province was once the private preserve of the Hudson's Bay Company. It takes pride in its role as gateway both to east and west and its capital, Winnipeg, the fourth largest city in Canada with a population of 600,000 is strategically placed only 170 miles (270 kilometres) from the geographical centre of the North American continent. America's border is 60 miles (95 kilometres) south, and Great Lakes port 450 miles (725 kilometres) to the east and Liverpool is less than 3,000 miles (4,800 kilometres) from the Port of Churchill on Hudson Bay which is 600 miles (965 kilometres) by rail north from Winnipeg. These minimal distances draw industries and commercial firms to the capital. Even the Golden Boy on top of Winnipeg's Legislative Building had more than his share of travelling before settling there.

The Golden Boy was commissioned in France before the First World War. Charles Gardet was the sculptor. The work was complete before Paris came under fire but a bomb damaged the factory where the gilded statue was waiting for shipment. Despite wartime difficulties he was loaded on a vessel about to cross the Atlantic. Unfortunately this was commandeered as a troop ship and the Golden Boy remained in her hold for the duration of the fighting, crossing and recrossing the Atlantic. However the ship survived and so did the statue which was eventually delivered to its rightful perch atop the 240 foot (73 metres) high dome overlooking the city. Of course he has a sheaf of wheat under one arm. Two sturdy bronze buffaloes flank the wide staircase of this building and other statues, not mythical, stand in the grounds including one of Queen Victoria. There is no entrance fee and you can visit between 9 a.m. and 4 p.m.

Winnipeg is Canada's rail centre particularly for meat and grain and her first locomotive, the 'Countess of Dufferin', the first steam engine to reach the west, has pride of place, gleaming like black satin, on Main Street, north of the Cultural Complex and City Hall.

Of the museums, that of Man and Nature is outstanding. Even as you arrive inside it appears that you do so on a space ship. Audio-visual presentations take you through the history of the province.

A visit to the Grain Exchange at 167 Lombard Avenue is a popular pastime and it is open during the week from 9.30 a.m. to 1.15 p.m. There is a visitors' gallery but, as with the cattle auctions in Calgary, the bargaining to the uninitiated sounds like exasperated men shouting at each other, although it is really good natured. Another unusual place to visit is the Winnipeg Mint where you can watch Canadian money being made. Presses work at a speed of 300 strokes a minute. Perhaps rimming is one of the most fascinating things to watch. A rim is formed to protect the designs and to allow finished coins to be stacked face to face.

Winnipeg has long been a main shopping centre for western Canada. Portage Avenue is lined with department stores and speciality shops. Polo Park, Garden City, Unity Fashion Square and streets crossing them are all tempting but the most famous intersection in this quarter is Portage and Main. Recently a six million dollar underground concourse was completed beneath it plus parking for 1,000 cars at the cost of another seven million dollars. The city council is considering making it illegal to cross this busy intersection at ground level and instead to divert pedestrians underground. Not that there will be any objection to this in the winter when the weather is bitterly cold and blizzards and snowstorms bring the temperature down well below zero. One explorer is said to have claimed that during the winter crossing Portage and Main can be worse than sledding in the Arctic.

The most impressive departmental store is Hudson's Bay Company, no great surprise as Winnipeg is not only the firm's headquarters but houses its archives. These had been kept in London since the seventeenth century when detailed reports were carried across the Atlantic in ships whose holds were crammed with furs. They recrossed the Atlantic in quite a different way in 1974, carefully packed in 20 ton aluminium containers. In 1939 when King George and Queen Elizabeth, the present Queen Mother, visited Winnipeg they were presented with the statutory tribute of the company to the reigning sovereign—the heads of two elks and two black beaver skins.

If you do not have the stamina to shop in large department stores there is the delightful area known as Osborne Village. Elegant boutiques and small shops sell everything from jewellery to exotic soaps, the latest fashions and antiques. There is a branch of Laura Ashley here with matching wallpaper fabrics and home furnishings. There is even a place called Floating Ecstasy where you can buy water beds, wicker furniture and bathroom novelties. Wrought-iron staircases lead you into tiny boutiques and window boxes are colourful. The inner man is not forgotten—there are discreet restaurants of different types from Basil's with light snacks, to Engl's with Tyrolean decor, Austrian food and Strauss music. We had dinner one night in a Victorian house which had been converted into a restaurant. My turtle soup was so delicious I asked if I might congratulate the chef. Hans Boog turned out to be Swiss from Lucerne. When I enquired about the turtle soup he readily gave me his recipe. Starting with the traditional turtle soup he adds a little oxtail soup, laces it with sherry, madeira and brandy and finishes with a small sprinkling of curry powder and a topping of whipped cream. No wonder it tastes so good!

Among the scarce culinary delights of the world is wild rice, so delicious to use in stuffing pheasant and partridge, if you can afford it, and a great treat also served with an exotic curry. Manitoba is one of the few sources of this delicacy and it is still gathered by the Indians who introduced it to the early fur traders and pioneers. The reason for its high cost and comparative rarity is its harvesting by paddling canoes through the swamps and threshing the ripe kernels into the bottom of the boat with two sticks.

There are some three hundred churches in Winnipeg ranging from the ultra-modern to St Boniface Bascilica, the oldest cathedral in western Canada. Unfortunately there have been several fires which have gutted it but the skeleton remains and a new smaller church has been built within its columned arches. It is somewhat incongruous to find a granite memorial to the rebel, Riel, but his body is buried in the churchyard and who is to say whether he was right or wrong.

The most popular annual event is the Festival of Nations, called Folklorama. Winnipeg has representative ethnic groups from all over Europe and at festival time there are more than twenty different pavilions each staffed by people wearing the appropriate national costume. They sell traditional food and entertain their guests with song and dance and you can buy handcrafted wares which cannot be obtained elsewhere. It is a colourful and happy event and it would take a week to sample everything.

If possible include Lower Fort Garry, some 20 miles (32 kilometres) north of Winnipeg, in your itinerary. If time is not of the essence for this expedition you have a choice of two types of craft on the Red river, either the normal sightseeing boat or a stern wheeler in the best Mark Twain tradition. If you drive go via Highway 9. The fort is open daily from 9 a.m. to 6 p.m. and the guides are in 1850 costume. Parking space is at present somewhat confined but will be ample in the future, as part of Highway 9 is to be diverted to make more room.

Lower Fort Garry is the only stone fort in western Canada which has survived in good condition. Small wonder when you see that the loopholed walls are 3 feet (1 metre) thick and 7½ feet (over 2 metres) high. They enclose about 4½ acres (almost 2 hectares). The south-east and north-east bastions were used as storage for powder and cannon balls and included a bakery and ice houses to keep food fresh.

The Governor's residence, a bungalow, is in the centre and has been restored to its original state. The barracks are by the west gate and housed the first troops of the North West Mounted Police the forerunners of the RCMP. The prison is on the north side, as is a retail store and a large furloft. The latter was in use until 1911 when lower Fort Garry ceased to be a trading post. The store has been turned into a museum which, among other bric-a-brac, displays pioneer rifles and ploughs. One of the best exhibits is an old York boat near the store by the south wall. Such spacious craft took men, pelts and goods along the western waterways in the old days.

Whiteshell Provincial Park 90 miles (145 kilometres) from Winnipeg on the Trans-Canada Highway covers an area of 1,065 square miles (2,758 square kilometres). Here you can fish, hunt or camp and the most popular place is Falcon Lake ski resort which also has tennis courts and an 18-hole golf course. There are over two hundred lakes teaming with trout, pike, walleye and bass.

The well-known places have lodges but some lakes which are rarely fished are accessible only by floatplane giving seclusion as well as a sense of adventure—but come to any of these places armed against large, vicious mosquitoes!

Manitoba has many mobile home parks which are generally open from mid-May until the end of September. They are well equipped and usually offer 'hook ups' which means plugging into mains water and electricity and sometimes even additional facilities.

5 TORONTO AND THE HEARTLAND OF CANADA

Toronto is a main gateway to central Canada for British visitors. Both Air Canada and British Airways fly direct from Heathrow and Prestwick. The flight takes under eight hours. If you collect a hired car from the airport the drive into town is fairly easy along a multi-lane highway gradually verging into the grid pattern of the city centre, so you have little trouble getting to your hotel. Parking is not impossible—only difficult, and the use of seat belts is mandatory in Ontario.

However blasé you have become about city towers with revolving restaurants, you cannot but be thrilled at your first glimpse of the CN (Canadian National) Tower, whose real function is to serve as an aerial mast for communications. It is not because it is twice as tall as the Eiffel Tower nor that it takes less than a minute to speed upward over 1,100 feet (335 metres) in its glass-encased lifts to the restaurant and viewing platform. It is because it is so unbelievably slender and elegant. The view from the top is exhilarating and gives you an idea of what you would like to see when back at ground level. On a clear day the city spreads like a carpet beneath highrise buildings and edges into the gleaming waters of Lake Ontario. You can see continuous movement of small aircraft at the local airfield on an island just off shore to remind you how much a country with Canada's distances depends on this form of transport. Minute coloured dots are moving vehicles and the tiny innumerable ones are trees. Toronto must be one of the few places where you can telephone the town hall for a man to come out and plant a tree in your garden, and not pay for it. In conditions of cloud if you are at the top of the tower you can have an aircraft-eye view in full sunshine while from below over half the tower can be invisible.

The mid-city plaza is a draw for both locals and visitors alike,

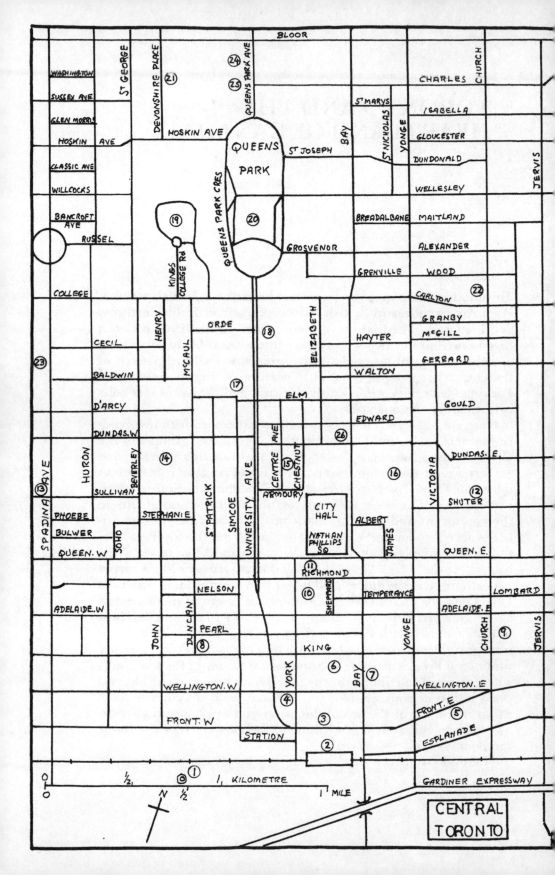

its focal point being the controversial City Hall. Five hundred and twenty architects from forty-two countries entered a competition to design it. An award jury selected eight finalists and on 26 September 1958 the Mayor Nathan Phillips QC, announced that a Finn from Helsinki, Viljo Reveil, had won. His design is certainly distinctive and dramatic, unlike any other town hall you have ever seen, yet fits in with the modern architecture in this section of Toronto.

The 'new' city hall (it still retains that title, the 'old' one being close by and now used for the courts) consists of two high curved tower blocks arranged like a pair of great interlaced commas with the council chamber as a full stop between them. Its cornerstone is equally novel being one of the concrete piles. The twenty-seventh floor of the east tower is open to the public and here you can get a closer but less spectacular view of the city than from the CN Tower. Also you can look down on the plaza itself and see the large rectangular pool which in winter is kept frozen and attracts lunchtime skaters. In summer it is jewelled with fountains and reflects some of the colourful flower boxes which are everywhere. When you are down at ground level once more you can tell the time by a large bronze sundial and puzzle over the name of one of Henry Moore's gigantic works called 'The Archer'.

There are pedestrian walkways with benches and other plazas with shallow staircases, always decorated with flower boxes and

TORONTO

Key to map

1	CN Tower	14	Art Gallery
2	Union Station	15	Chinatown
3	Airport Bus Terminal/	16	Toronto Eaton Centre
	Royal York Hotel	17	New Mount Sinai Hospital
4	Strathcona Hotel	18	Toronto General Hospital
5	St Lawrence Centre	19	University of Toronto
6	Toronto Dominion Centre	20	Parliament Buildings
7	Commerce Court	21	Varsity Stadium and Arena
8	Royal Alexandra Theatre	22	Maple Leaf Gardens. Ice Hockey
9	St James Cathedral	23	Kensington Market
10	The Lanes	24	Royal Ontario Museum
11	Sheraton Centre	25	McLaughlin Planetarium
12	St Michael's Cathedral	26	Bus Terminal
13	China Court Shopping Centre		

urns, all within walking distance. They lead to fascinating places such as the 'new' Eaton Centre, a truly enormous glass-enclosed shopping complex, which gives on to a galleria of other shops; the whole is so big it brings to mind London's Crystal Palace, of the last century. You can shop on ten floors and there is still room for offices. There are two street-level restaurants, the Dundas Room and The Patio (both licensed) and four other cafés. Eaton's is a nationwide chain (they have seven other stores in the Toronto area) founded by one, Timothy Eaton, and in this latest department store many of the old customs are carried on. He decreed when he opened his first shop that tobacco must not be sold and the rule still holds. An annual Santa Claus parade is now traditional. A famous bronze statue of Timothy Eaton on a plinth has been re-sited inside the entrance of the new complex. This has given birth to a new custom in which shoppers, whenever they separate while shopping, invariably meet each other again 'under Tim's toe!'

Simpson's and Eaton's have been competitors for over a century and most Canadians would think it eccentric to shop in one without visiting the other. Schoolchildren continue to laugh at the old adage which started when Eaton's and Simpson's became rivals— 'Eaton can do without Simpson but Simpson can't do without eatin'!'

Leaving the galleria at the Trinity Way exit you come upon two historic buildings that are protected; Trinity Church, which used to be one of the city's most prominent landmarks, and Scadding House. The twin church spires were used by sailors on Lake Ontario to take their bearings in the 1800s. The nineteenth-century Scadding House used to act as a community centre serving meals to downtown office workers. Today making room for Eaton Centre, it has been shifted some 150 feet (45 metres) and the approach is through a passage way. Close by, at the corner of Queen and Yonge and declared a historic site, stands one of the oldest Simpson stores. When it was opened in 1894 it was described as 'the finest building of its kind in Canada.' It has been extensively renovated inside recently but retains its 'Chicago'-style ambience.

Not to be outdone by Simpson and Eaton, Hudson's Bay have their emporium firmly anchored at the corner of Yonge and Bloor Streets and, of course, there are thousands of people who would not shop elsewhere but at 'The Bay'. Where, for instance, could you get anything to touch those warm, softly coloured, pure wool Hudson's Bay blankets, or even such artistic Eskimo carvings?

Many of the country's largest banks and insurance companies

are centred in Toronto's modern plazas and four, bearing the names of the nation's leading banks, seem to be the highest buildings and are close together. The Bank of Montreal's monolith, seventy-two storeys encased in white Italian marble, is the tallest and there are the fifty-seven-floor stainless-steel Commerce Court, the three tall blocks of the Toronto Dominion Centre and the twin towers of the Royal Bank, the latter glistening gold on a sunny day—and that is just what it is since gold was used in the glazing to impart heat and glare-reflecting qualities. Its underground shopping concourse has a magnificent fountain and is guarded by closed circuit TV. The ground-level area of one of these plazas has a unique system of blinds, thermostatically controlled to cover the glass roof when the sun beats down and so reduce the temperature within.

Eventually all these mid-town plazas will have their own shopping malls joined together underground and provide access to Union Station in the south, York Centre in the west and City Hall in the north. In all, troglodyte Toronto will have eight city blocks beneath the ground with strolling, shopping and dining, two hotels, three cinemas and three subway stops. Going to the other extreme nearly all the highrise buildings have observation galleries, restaurants and snack bars in the clouds.

Hotel accommodation is no problem in Toronto. It is said there is something to suit every pocket and that there are over 20,000 hotel and motel rooms in the metropolitan area. Incidentally, 'Metro Toronto' is a federation of the heart of the city and five boroughs with about two million residents.

Despite recent de luxe hotels the Royal York, a CP undertaking built in 1929 for the then unheard sum of 20 million dollars, is still the queen of them all—and determined to stay that way. Its site is perfect for it is opposite Toronto's Union Station yet connected underground to the shopping area beneath Royal Bank Plaza. Like its sister chateaux the Royal York is not just thought of as a hotel but as an institution.

Although I travelled a good deal with my parents as a schoolgirl, I remember the first time I stayed at the Royal York when my father was amused because I was so impressed with its size. Today I am even more impressed for, to retain its title of 'City within a City', it has expanded out of recognition and can now host 1,400 people for a banquet, 2,200 for a meeting and provide dinner for up to 2,000 people attending a convention which arrives at individual tables at exactly the right temperature. The elevators have the same wood panelling I remember—but there are many more of them. The Acadian Room as always has its oak beams and gleaming copper pans. Antique furniture is still lovingly polished and there are the same deep, capacious chairs in the foyer—only now my feet reach the floor! For guests who want something up to the minute there are trendy boutiques, colour TV sets which also show a selection of the latest movies and a double spiral staircase which adds a glamorous touch for it was the first to be installed in North America.

There is no doubt that the hotel chains take on personalities of their own. Sheraton is one which keeps its image alive although it makes a point of reflecting each country's particular features. In Cairo the dining room has leather walls tooled with gilt and exquisite *mushrabia* (wooden latticework) screens. The word 'Sheraton' though of Western origin, is connected by chance with ancient Egypt for it was the name of Pharaoh Akhnaten's daughter —*Sher* meaning little and *Aton* meaning sun so the name is inscribed in hieroglyphics over the hotel entrance. In Tunisia the Sheraton Hotel in Hammamet adheres to the rule that no hotel must rise above the height of a palm tree so it sprawls, in oriental style, with hidden and unusual terraces. The Sheraton Centre fits into the Toronto scene in exactly the opposite way—by soaring into the air for over forty storeys like other high rise buildings. From our room on the thirty-fifth floor we had a most wonderful view of the CN tower at night when it looked like a thin silver lance piercing the dark velvet sky. The Sheraton Centre contains its own shopping village with more than thirty-five shops and boutiques on three levels, and to forget the bustle of city centre life for a while, guests can stroll through landscaped gardens or watch the waterfall in the foyer rushing into its wishing pool. The inevitable coins tossed into it are given to charity. The waterfall is enhanced by several pheasants which strut about displaying their brilliant plumage. Although their wings are lightly clipped to prevent them from escaping, a telephone call one morning alerted the management that a covey of pheasants were sauntering along the pavement outside the hotel. As Sheraton Centre is just opposite the City Hall plaza such a strange sight was bound to tie up the busy traffic. The birds were retrieved and it was discovered later that they had hopped up one side of the waterfall and as their feathers had grown again had managed to flutter outside the entrance where they preened themselves in front of delighted but incredulous on-lookers.

St James Anglican Cathedral of yellow brick was built in 1853 over the site of two previous churches which burned down. Its steeple is Canada's tallest and took twenty years to finish. Little Trinity Church (not to be confused with Trinity Church outside Eaton Centre) was built for Irish Protestants of limited means who could not afford to pay the pew rents in the cathedral. It is the oldest in Toronto. St Michael's Cathedral, completed in 1848 is Roman Catholic. Its 260 foot (79 metre) spire is unique in that it has a fragment of the True Cross embedded in it, 'sent from Rome by the Holy Father as a token of his affection for the Metropolis of English Canada.'

Yorkville village is a charming shopping area consisting of Cumberland Street, Yorkville Avenue, Hazelton Avenue and Scollard Street. Like Gastown in Vancouver during the 'flower-power hippie era', it was a sleazy district but again like Gastown it is a completely different story now. Some say that the building of the Four Seasons Hotel at the corner of Yorkville and Avenue Road started the revitalization. Now it is one of the liveliest and most pleasant places to stroll, take an outdoor meal under shady trees and watch the world go by. It has several art galleries, speciality shops, boutiques, restaurants and outdoor cafés. Close by is the Royal Ontario Museum, referred to affectionately as 'Rom'. About twenty galleries are given over to a fantastic Chinese collection, the finest in the country.

Just south of the museum and its adjoining McLaughlin Planetarium, is the campus of Toronto University which has 55,000 students. Here you can glimpse its ivy-covered buildings, wooded walkways and green lawns. Insulin was discovered here, and the pacemaker which has helped so many people with heart troubles to lead a normal life, was invented.

There's a touching, and often ignored, little monument on the opposite corner. It's dedicated to Edith Cavell and the Canadian nurses who gave their lives in the first Great War. It is in a most suitable place as, within this relatively small area, are some of the city's most famous hospitals.

Crossing University Avenue is Dundas Street, the heart of Toronto's Chinatown, with all the exotic sights, sounds and smells of the East. Here you can visit Oriental shops and restaurants, and grocery shopping can be quite an adventure. Further west along Dundas Street stands the low, massive pile of the Art Gallery of Ontario, with the most up-to-date facilities for displaying the extensive collections and constantly changing 'on loan' exhibits.

Don't miss the recently opened wing devoted to all phases of Canadian art. It also has a large Henry Moore collection.

Casa Loma, Toronto's famous castle, should be seen even if you only drive by it. It was built with ninety-eight rooms, between 1911 and 1914 by Sir Henry Pellatt, soldier, financier, industrialist and an incurable romantic who was fascinated by medieval castles. Having accumulated a great fortune he decided to build one himself. Marble, glass and panelling were brought from Europe, and Scottish stonemasons crossed the Atlantic to make the great wall that surrounds it. Spanish tiles and the best mahogany were used to line the stables where the finest horses were kept. One hallway is a replica of that at Windsor Castle. The panelling of the lovely Oak Room took three years to carve. There are luxurious suites and a secret staircase. From the battlements, with their far-reaching views, to the wine cellars you feel the whole place might have existed in the Middle Ages. Sir Henry and Lady Pellatt lived there until the 1920s when even his fortune could no longer keep the place going so, under an agreement, the Kiwanis Club of west Toronto took it over as a tourist attraction and use their share of the proceeds to support certain community projects.

Not far from Chinatown there are several narrow streets known as Kensington Market. Despite its dignified name there are frontless shops, pavement stalls and bargaining in different languages with much flailing of arms and good-natured banter as people haggle over prices. If the Middle Eastern style bargaining does not appeal to you, you can buy just about anything from ordinary shops which are spotlessly clean and display enticing meats, fish, vegetables and fruit. Quail and chicken are sold 'on the hoof' and you either have their necks wrung on the spot or take them home alive and cope with them yourself. Strange smells assail the nostrils on every side and there are very exotic cheeses to be had. Kensington Market is a polyglot quarter which is always crowded with locals and amused tourists—especialy on Saturdays.

The Ontario Science Centre is a place you must visit if you are interested in the future and intrigued with ultra-modern devices which may be a mystery to you. The actual building itself is like no other and the architect, Raymond Moriyam, designed it to appear part of a canyon. The entrance is at 770 Don Mills Road. Once inside and having paid $1.50 for your ticket, you take glass-sided escalators, connected by glass-enclosed ramps, and travel down the side of a ravine with landscaped views either side. In the valley you enter three different halls which are full of futuristic devices which you are bidden to touch, feel and examine and thereby gauge the extent to which present-day life is based on science and technology. You could spend days in this extraordinary place and it is impossible to enumerate the various exhibits. But to mention a few: you can test your reflexes, your perception, your fitness, make music, challenge the wits of a computer, land on the moon in a simulator, start your own show in a theatre, manipulate mechanical hands, be conductor for an electric current which literally makes your hair stand on end. There are more than 550 different things to do and see in the three buildings.

To bring you back to normal life there are other places to visit. Just to the east of Toronto University there is Queen's Park, named after Queen Victoria, where aged trees and green lawns surround the rose-tinted, Romanesque Ontario Parliament Buildings. Should you care to listen to the parliamentary procedure first hand, drop in to the 'bear pit' sessions—more commonly referred to as question period, between 2-3 p.m. when the Legislature is in session. From the steps of the Parliament Buildings you can see University Avenue, one of Toronto's main thoroughfares. The startling concave structure on the west corner, reflecting the surrounding buildings off its mirrored surface, is the new 45 million dollar headquarters of Ontario Hydro. It has a radical heating system, which eliminates the traditional furnace, and recycles 30 per cent of the energy expended. Ask any Torontonian and he'll tell you it uses solar energy but surprisingly this is not true. Heat is provided by the interior lighting and the actual warmth of the people in the building which is carefully husbanded by insulation and inward reflection.

Ontario Place, some 4 miles (6 kilometres) westward along the lake is a place to relax for both young and old. Half built out over the water it covers nearly 100 acres (40 hectares), one part being a children's village with all kinds of amusements often referred to as 'Disneyland on Stilts'! It also has pavilions, theatres and a 900-seat Cinesphere where you can see films about Canadian life in the past and today. Small pleasure craft bob up and down along a marina, there are picnic areas and there is an outdoor amphitheatre called the Forum. Another part of the waterfront consists of old wharves and docks filled in and covered with boutiques, markets and a wide array of restaurants.

Fort York is close by Ontario Place and was the British Army headquarters in 1812 when Toronto was called York. In April of that year an American armed force came ashore a mile or so away and attacked the town of York. To prevent barrels of gunpowder falling into enemy hands the British blew them up thereby killing and wounding many of the invading force who then proceeded to burn down the Parliament Buildings. It was in retaliation for this that the British were later to burn down the White House when they marched on Washington.

Fort York has been reconstructed and is open throughout the year. It has eight buildings and during the summer men dressed in the uniforms of those stirring days march and counter march to the sounds of fife and drum and perform other duties like the soldiers of the early nineteenth century.

Toronto is full of restaurants and the variety is such that you can easily find what you want whether it is a quick inexpensive snack, a medium priced meal or a candle-lit dinner with all the trimmings. Most of them accept the major credit cards. The Sheraton Centre has the Café of the Redwoods where you can order a 'Taste of Canada' menu. Among the desserts you must not miss maple syrup mousse—it certainly could not be more Canadian and it tastes delicious—but more of food in another chapter.

Toronto parks are numerous as in most Canadian cities and there is something I shall always remember about them—signs read 'Please walk on the grass'.

The McMichael Canadian Collection is within easy reach of Toronto in the village of Kleinburg some 20 miles (32 kilometres) north-west of the city. Most of the Group of Seven came from Toronto and there are some 700 works by them and their contemporaries housed in a series of low timber and stone galleries in parkland. There is no admission charge and the collection is open to the public every afternoon (except Mondays) and most public holidays throughout the year. It is the largest permanent display of Thomson's pictures to be seen anywhere and the studio shack in which he painted many of his masterpieces has been re-erected in the gallery grounds. There are thirty gallery rooms in all displaying not only works by Emily Carr, David Milne and Clarence Gagnon but several superb carvings and paintings by Eskimo and Indian artists. You can have lunch or tea in the quiet pine-panelled dining room.

From Toronto an out-of-town excursion with an appealing Indian background is Sainte-Marie-among-the-Hurons at Midland, where you can visit a true-to-life reconstruction of a Jesuit mission trading post enclosed by a palisade. It has been rebuilt so painstakingly that you can imagine the paddling of canoes along the stream which edges the encampment and you can see a film depicting life in the 1600s.

The Hurons were entrepreneurs. Leading a settled agricultural life, they acted as middlemen, being shrewd traders and knowing full well that furs could be exchanged for things of such value to the Indians as metal arrowheads, fish hooks, knives and hatchets. The Jesuits thought their Christian missionary work might best be begun with a tribe of Indians who preferred to remain in one place rather than one of the nomadic tribes. So gradually Sainte Marie grew into quite a large mission with church, hospital, dwellings and a 'longhouse' for meetings.

The fatal flaw was that the Hurons' traditional enemies were the Iroquois who decided to break up the Huron French alliance. Sainte-Marie continued to flourish and became the central post for five missions which by 1649 had grown to twelve. Many of the Hurons in the meantime had become Christians, won over by the fact that the priests among them wished to give and not to take. Unfortunately the Frenchmen had brought their European diseases with them such as smallpox and tuberculosis so that the Hurons were soon sadly decimated. Up to this point the Iroquois had been content with sporadic raids. These now increased and in the early spring of 1648, by a surprise attack while the snow was still on the ground, they massacred 2,000 Hurons. The Jesuits refused to leave their flock and suffered losses also. In 1649 more mission villages were razed and two Jesuits, Father Brebeuf and Father Lalemant, were taken prisoners and tortured to death. Later six other priests suffered the same fate. At a serious pow-wow in the longhouse it was decided by the remaining priests and Hurons to move some 20 miles (32 kilometres) away to an island which came to be called Christian Island. The many years of work at Sainte-Marie had come to an end and the whole mission was burned to prevent it falling into Iroquois hands. As one priest was to write, 'We ourselves set fire to it, and beheld it burn before our eyes.' The eight Jesuit priests who had been murdered were later canonized by the Roman Catholic Church and today a Martyrs' Shrine is kept by the Jesuits and stands across the road from the reconstructed Sainte-Marie-among-the-Hurons.

Barrie, some 56 miles (90 kilometres) from Toronto along Highway 400 leads to the 30 mile (48 kilometre) lake Simcoe where the county museum shows displays of pioneer life, and there are lovely picnic areas. It is always intriguing to see houses where famous people lived and at Orillia further on is the mansion of the great Canadian humourist Stephen Leacock. His library is particularly interesting, being a hodge-podge of the sort of books one collects oneself. Perhaps, as he was a professor at McGill University, his room there had a more orthodox book selection.

Gravenhurst is about 25 miles (40 kilometres) from Orillia and is probably best known in, of all places, China, because another famous Canadian, a doctor this time, was born there, one Norman Bethune. He became well known for his medical aid to Mao Tse Tung's army in the early days of the long march and he died tending them. His house, now also a museum, has become a must for any Chinese visitor. Gravenhurst is a gateway to the Muskoka Lakes, one of Ontario's finest holiday regions, and has acted as such since the Victorian era. It retains many buildings of the period including an opera house which has recently been renovated, complete with air conditioning. A summer stock company is resident in July and August and gives plays and musicals. Another summer tradition is that every Sunday evening there is a band concert from a stage built out over Gull Lake.

We were told by the Mayoress, Wanda Miller, that, when the Queen and Prince Philip visited there recently, instead of the usual bouquet of flowers from a local shop, a bunch of local wild flowers was carefully collected and that the Queen was delighted with this unusual presentation.

Further on, the Muskoka Lakes, large and small, are dotted about with summer cottages and tourist lodges with small landing stages for boats, for this is a great holiday region. In the winter there is skating and the longest skiing season in Ontario running from December to mid-April.

The place which your adventurous type of holiday maker really loves in Ontario is the enormous, wild Algonquin Park, one of the largest in the country. By government decree it is 'left to nature', an ideal retreat for canoeist, camper and fisherman. One forest ranger told me that when he first left school he arranged to go there camping with some friends and they had flown to a remote lake by floatplane. The pilot waved goodbye and said he would fetch them in a week from the same spot. They put up their tent, hung their supplies up neatly inside and went off fishing. When they returned in the evening ready to have a camp fire and a good meal with grilled fish, bread, beans and cheese they found to their annoyance that bears had either eaten or made off with their week's supplies. Luckily they had one box of matches and they enjoyed the freshly grilled fish. During the week that followed they got heartily sick of fish and wild berries which was all they had to eat and they became as thin as male models. 'No pilot was ever more welcome than ours when he came to pick us up the following week,' the forest ranger finished ruefully.

Starting yet again from the hub, Toronto (which incidentally is the Indian word for 'meeting place'), you can set off in a westerly direction this time for Stratford 100 miles (160 kilometres) away. We found it one of the highlights of our Ontario tour and reminiscent of England. It is of course famous for its annual Shakespeare Festival and it would not have surprised us to see William Shakespeare himself walking by the river. Considerable trouble has been taken to reproduce the charm and atmosphere of its English forerunner without slavish imitation. True, it does have its splendid theatre set in 150 acres (60 hectares) on the banks of the River Avon, complete with sweeping lawns and gliding swans, but it also has its own individuality.

Every effort has been made within an ultra-modern setting to reproduce the type of theatre for which Shakespeare wrote his plays. Chichester Theatre in England was copied from it. Tyrone Guthrie designed the stage; scenery is of the simplest but the emphasis is on costume. Its 2,258 seats are banked about the jutting semi-circular stage, in such a way that no one is more than 65 feet (20 metres) away. Every new aid including close-circuit TV, infrared light, booths for control of light, sound and stage management, are set above and behind the audience and the lighting control is computerized. The audience feels it is part of the play and actors come on to the stage through tunnels beneath the auditorium and indeed often down the radiating aisles. The stage is surrounded by a waist-high moat, called the 'gutter', in which actors await their cues unobtrusively.

The Stratford Festival has been an astounding success for over 26 years and tickets are as difficult to get as for a Nureyev ballet. We were fortunate enough to be shown around the theatre by Barry MacGregor, an actor manager. I asked him not to tell us about the productions which are so well written up by the critics but to tell us some of the amusing things that have happened—which he did.

When they wish to get many actors onto the stage quickly, as in a battle scene, they use the aisles as well as the tunnels beneath the auditorium. It is all too easy in the dim light of a scene change for an unrehearsed incident to occur. One knight collected a lady's hat on his way and when the lights came up it was perched on top of his halberd! Often the audience's asides are heard by the actors. 'Oh,' screamed one elderly lady to her companion, 'isn't it fun being in the middle of the battle!' Another lady felt one of the actor's silken cloaks, saying to her husband, 'This is the same material Mary has for her new dress!'

Things happen on the stage sometimes that are not in the script, such as the performance when Ophelia was being lowered into her tomb through the stage trap door and one of the monks tripped and fell in after her. 'The only thing we could do,' said Barry laughing, 'was to shut the trap door. It was probably the only time that necrophelia has come into a Shakespearean play!'

Barry's most amusing anecdote concerned himself. He was just about to step onto the stage from the 'gutter' one night when his cloak got caught. He gave a tug but could not release it. He tried again and still seemed trapped. Glancing backward he saw a very pretty girl holding onto the hem. 'What is your 'phone number?' she asked quickly. He just managed to get his cloak loose and take his cue and while telling us began to laugh. 'Guess what we were playing?' he asked.

'I've no idea,' I said.

'She Stoops to Conquer!'

From Stratford you can return eastwards but rather than go back to Toronto, keep along the south shore of Lake Ontario and you will pass through one of the prolific Canadian vineyard areas. In addition this is one of the fruit-growing sections in Ontario but it is unexpected to drive for miles along the Niagara Peninsula almost believing yourself to be in Bordeaux or the Neckar Valley. The vines are grown to exactly the same height as those in France or Germany and are as lovingly tended. Indeed the original stock for these vines came from Europe. By a quirk of fate when the dreaded phylloxera, the most serious of all vine diseases, swept through the European vineyards at the turn of the century, the only way of halting the disease was to burn all the vines there, and stock from California and Ontario was brought back again across the Atlantic to restart European viticulture.

Of the Canadian wine companies probably Brights is the best known. It was founded in 1874. The original buildings and cellars are still used along with modern warehouses. We found a tour of the winery most interesting. Tours are available year-round, Monday to Friday at various scheduled times between the hours of 9.30 a.m. and 3.30 p.m., and there is no charge.

Further east along the peninsula, on the opposite side of Lake

Ontario to Toronto, you come to Niagara Falls (from Toronto it is 80 miles (130 kilometres). This must be one of the greatest tourist attractions in the world and even more photographed than Lake Louise. Famous comments about it are legion. Oscar Wilde said it would be a 'wonder if the water fell up,' and then there is the Yorkshireman who was shown the falls and told how many millions of gallons per second flowed over. He replied, 'Ay. Ah see nowt to stop it!' No matter what people say, nothing can take away from the magnificence of the falls and at night, when they are illuminated with coloured beams, you might well be in a Hans Christian Andersen fairytale land. The American side appears to be more highly commercialized but on the Canadian side a delightful parkland takes over, although in the town a slightly bizarre atmosphere is created by Ripley's Believe It or Not, the House of Frankenstein and other emporia such as Boris Karloff and Houdini. One can only presume that such places are at Niagara because they are about as unlikely as the falls themselves. It has always been a great place for honeymoon couples though the film directors who make movies about it never even ask how it came about. It is alleged that Napoleon's brother brought his bride here by coach from New Orleans in 1804 and perhaps this may have started the fashion which has now gone on for over a century. Oscar Wilde had a second sardonic comment about Niagara, saying that seeing the falls after the first night of the honeymoon must have been the bride's 'second great disappointment.' However the vogue started, hotels and motels do a roaring trade and vie with each other over the facilities offered.

The falls themselves are awe-inspiring and beautiful and there are several exciting ways to see them. You can fly above them in a helicopter, ride upwards some 520 feet (158 metres) in an external glass-enclosed elevator on the skylon tower gazing into the thundering foam or dine in its revolving restaurant. You can take the 'Maid of the Mist', a sturdy little ship for half an hour's trip on the turbulent water where the noise is deafening and you are handed raincoats to keep you dry from the spray. What I found most impressive of all was going down in an elevator through the rock to the gorge below the falls to a walkway that takes you along the edge of the rapids to the famous whirlpool. Whenever you see the falls in the sunshine, rainbows are formed in the spray.

The Niagara Parkway runs 35 miles (56 kilometres) along the waterway connecting Lakes Ontario and Erie including the falls themselves, and is a very pleasant drive. You can go direct to

Niagara-on-the-Lake at the very edge of Ontario due south across the water from Toronto, from which city it can also be reached by boat. At Niagara-on-the-Lake a restrained and authentic restoration job has been done to reproduce a nineteenth century small town. Families have lived in many of the houses for decades and the great annual event is the Shaw Festival which started fifteen years ago. In Main Street you will find an Apothecary Shop, operating since 1835 and the Fudge Shop where you can buy home-made candy and, if you happen to be there at the right time, watch the fudge being made.

East from Toronto along the Lake Ontario is Kingston, founded by Count Frontenac in 1673. Its main attraction is Old Fort Henry built three centuries ago and well restored. From spring to autumn cadets give displays of nineteenth-century gun drill, provide a fife and drum band and on Wednesdays and Saturdays they beat the retreat at 7.30 p.m. Perhaps because of these stirring displays and the fact that Kingston was capital of Canada in 1840 the town has a pleasant, long-settled atmosphere.

Bellevue House has also become a popular place for tourists to visit. Guides are dressed in period costume and the well-kept garden produces the same flowers, vegetables and tobacco as it did during the 1840s when John A. MacDonald spent a year there. It was built some time prior to this by a wealthy grocer when it was nicknamed 'Tea Caddy Castle'. Unfortunately, during John MacDonalds's time there things went badly for him. His infant son died four weeks after he moved in, his wife was in delicate health and had to remain on the ground floor and his legal practice slumped to such an extent that he could no longer afford to remain and had to leave Bellevue House.

Who doubts that houses are lucky or unlucky? No matter what one believes it is strange that when MacDonald left Bellevue House in 1857 he went on to become one of the chief architects of Confederation, a leader of the Conservative Party, was knighted by Queen Victoria and finally became the first prime minister of Canada.

The domed City Hall, built while Kingston was the capital, is of limestone and one of the outstanding classical buildings in the country. Thirty-six feet (11 metres) high limestone martello towers were built for defence between 1845-8. Indeed, about this time, Kingston was one of the strongest fortresses in Canada. The martello towers were an early type of coastal fortification first thought to have been used by Charles V in Italy. Later they were

1 Totem poles in Stanley Park, Vancouver, British Columbia

2 Steam clock in Gastown, Vancouver, British Columbia. Power is provided from an underground heating main. Note the Victorian-type street lights

3 Skiing on Grouse Mountain, Vancouver, British Columbia

4 The Parliament Building of Victoria, Vancouver Island, British Columbia

5 A beaver lodge at Vermilion Lake, Banff, Alberta

6 Trail riders in Waterton Lakes National Park, Alberta

7 Banff Springs Hotel, Alberta, in winter

8 The shortest international bridge in the world – Zavikon Islands – Canadian on the left, American on the right, in the Thousands Islands section of the St Lawrence river, Ontario

9 A mock-Victorian general store in Upper Canada Village, Ontario

10 The Canadian National Tower, 1815 feet (553 metres) high, Toronto, Ontario

11 An amazing Toronto skyview, Ontario

12 Horseshoe falls at Niagara, Ontario

13 *Left* The dome of the library, Parliament Building, seen from the Peace Tower and overlooking the Ottawa river, Ontario

14 *Below* McGill station, Montreal, Quebec. The stations of the city's subway system are enlivened by murals, sculptures, stained-glass windows and ceramics

15 The twin-towered Notre Dame church in Montreal, Quebec

16 The Olympic Stadium in Montreal, Quebec

17 Chateau Frontenac Hotel in Quebec

18 Lockheed Hudson bomber monument to the wartime Atlantic ferry
pilots at Gander, Newfoundland

19 Evangeline statue at Grand Pré, Nova Scotia

20 The fortress of Louisbourg, Nova Scotia
21 The garden of the fortress of Louisbourg, Nova Scotia. Note the costumes of the attendants

22 Hopewell Cape rocks, New Brunswick. The little boy, barely visible, is minute in comparison

built along England's Channel coast when it was feared Napoleon would invade Britain. You can see the remaining ones in Kent today, and the island of Malta has some fourteen around its shores. Only one remains in Kingston, overlooking Lake Ontario close by Bellevue House and across from the City Hall. The loopholes at the base at one time provided cover for the ditch surrounding it. Today it is a museum which is open during the summer.

About the same time as the martello towers were built, Queen's University received its charter and churches were built including St George's Cathedral in King Street which became the seat of the first Bishop of Ontario. Its architecture is reminiscent of Wren's London churches.

There are several other places in Kingston to visit and the best (and rather unusual) way to see everything is to take the 'Tour Train'. This is a string of open carriages drawn by a tractor which goes around the streets on pneumatic wheels rather than running along a railway. On a summer's day it is a pleasant way to see the city and you can board it south of City Hall. It does eight trips daily taking you around the sights for some ten miles (16 kilometres). You will pass by the Royal Military College, Canada's Sandhurst, and several other places which you may wish to return to later and visit in your own time. Two exceptional buildings are the Pumphouse Steam Museum which claims to be the only one displaying its engines actually operating by steam, and the International Hockey Hall of Fame.

Canadian ice-hockey players are famous all over the world and it is a standing joke that many American teams are largely made up of Canadians. The American reply to this is that Canadian baseball teams are usually all American! You can see equipment and memorabilia recalling the history of ice hockey from its beginning in Kingston in 1885 up to the present day. There is a splendid collection of photographs and it is amusing to see how the clothing for the sport has changed.

From Kingston Lake Ontario flows into the long winding St Lawrence River and also into the southern end of the Rideau Canal which leads to Ottawa. A Thousand Islands' Boat Tour is as important as seeing Niagara Falls and each stretch of the river is more attractive than the last. There is a considerable choice of vessel even extending to a three-deck paddle wheeler. Kingston waterfront is picturesque and most of the islands present a different aspect, many of them being privately owned. One holds church services on Sundays from a rock pulpit while the congregation cluster round in boats; another is nearly covered by a large castle. Some have tropical trees and plants on their sunny side and hardier conifers on the other. You cruise along narrow channels and shallow waterways with views on either side. On the larger boats you can stroll along the decks and have a meal or a drink. Certainly you will not get sea sick but if boats do not appeal there are plane trips over the islands. Gananoque is a nearby resort and a boarding point for tours by boat or plane. Before the white man came, the Indians paddled their canoes among the many islands. The name is an old Indian one and means 'land which slopes towards the water and disappears.'

The three greatest draws in Ontario without question are Toronto, Niagara Falls and Ottawa. Queen Victoria chose Ottawa as Canada's capital. It was a shrewd diplomatic move which shocked many people at the time but disposed of any argument as to the prior claims of Toronto, Montreal or Kingston. It can be compared with the setting up of Washington as the 'neutral' capital of the United States. When it was selected it was an insignificant place called Bytown after its founder, a colonel of that name who built the Rideau Canal. It is sited on the Ottawa river near the Gatineau Hills with their forests and lakes. Its famous Parliament Buildings with their jade-coloured turrets and spires stand on a bluff over-looking the river opposite the French-speaking city of Hull.

The three Gothic buildings that house the Canadian parliament are surrounded by green lawns and many statues including one of Sir John A. MacDonald unveiled in 1895 to the accompaniment of a twenty-one gun salute. The centre block where the Senate and Commons meet is open to the public. The east and west blocks and the library, which you can also visit, are the original buildings of a century ago but the centre block was burned down in 1916 and replaced by a larger building. The library stands by itself and when the fire started it was hurriedly closed and luckily escaped. Its architecture reminds one of the back of Notre Dame Cathedral on the Ile de la Cité in Paris with its finnials and fretted work.

The soaring Peace Tower once know as Victory Tower, is about 300 feet (90 metres) high and is dedicated to the Canadians who died in the First World War. A page is turned each day in the Book of Remembrance which contains all their names.

During the summer from mid-June there is the Changing of the Guard ceremony every morning at 10.00 a.m. in front of the buildings by the Canadian Grenadier Guards in black bearskins and scarlet jackets, reminiscent of those at Buckingham Palace.

The hall of the House of Commons is in limestone and oak with green upholstered chairs. The Senate glows with crimson and gold. Of the many portraits of famous people, one of Queen Victoria has a strange history. She is portrayed as a young woman wearing a low-cut silken gown and jewellery, but only when it was pointed out to me did I realize that one arm was a little shorter than the other. This was in fact the case but she objected to statues and paintings where it was shown, so the portrait may be unique and this has survived several adventures. First when it was hung in Montreal's Parliament Building which burned down, it was one of the few paintings saved and, when it was moved to Ottawa and the central block burned down, it was away being cleaned.

A white light shows on top of the Peace Tower when Parliament is in session. There is an eternal flame fed by gas which bubbles up through the water in a pool, surrounded by the coats of arms of all the provinces on the front lawn. It was lit in 1967 as a symbol of Canada's century of nationhood and all the coins tossed into it are given to charity.

One of the things that strikes a quick response with people from Britain is the Canadian love of flowers. Despite truly icy weather, when winter is over, flower beds and boxes appear with daffodils and other spring flowers. Much of this magic is provided by the grateful Dutch. Queen Juliana of Holland spent some time during the last world war in Canada with her daughters and Princess Margriet, the youngest, was born in Ottawa. Since then tulip bulbs are sent to the Canadian capital each spring. Added to these, thousands of other bulbs are coaxed to life in May and, although so much further north, Ottawa suddenly vies with Washington during cherry-blossom time.

One of the delightful things about Ottawa being a small capital, even with 300,000 inhabitants, is that so much is within walking distance. Just across from Parliament Buildings is Sparke Street Mall, closed to motor vehicles and providing branches of all the well-known shops within an elegant walking precinct with fountains, flower urns and benches.

Just to the east of 'The Hill', as the site of Parliament Buildings is called, is the Rideau Canal linking with Kingston 100 miles (160 kilometres) away. It is edged with parkland, bicycle paths, flower beds and shrubs. Boatmen wait in case you wish to go on a water trip. Close by, looking as if it were part of the Parliament Buildings, stands the Chateau Laurier Hotel. The manager told us that people often come in through the entrance and ask whose castle it is or if

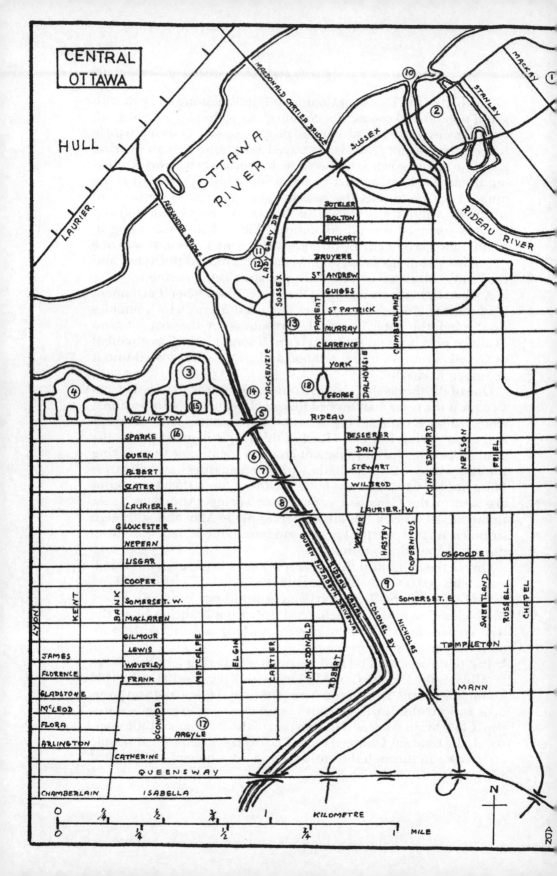

they might take a tour over it. Others seeing its turrets and jade-green roofing ask if the Prime Minister lives there.

Built of granite and limestone, the Chateau Laurier was named after Canada's eighth prime minister, Sir Wilfred Laurier, and was opened in 1912 with about 300 rooms. Down through the years it has housed kings and queens, presidents and senators, movie stars and diplomats. The suites and rooms are high, individually furnished and with walk-in wardrobes, but all with air conditioning and colour television. As the management says, 'we give the comforts of yesterday with the convenience of today.' There are banqueting halls and dining rooms and a large heated swimming pool. Your every wish appears to be anticipated and in the food line nothing seems impossible. There are things to eat which you have never heard of, such as strawberry flambé with pepper sauce, a piquant dish. I was interested to hear how it was made and like many delicious things it happened by accident. The chef had made what he called 'strawberry delight' and by mistake a sous chef had sprinkled black pepper on it. Instead of throwing them away, as it was the beginning of the strawberry season and they were expensive, the chef tasted the concoction and enjoyed it. It has been on the menu ever since and is a great favourite.

Ottawa looks beautiful enough floodlit at night with its masses of flowers, the Rideau Canal, the locks, the Gothic Parliament Buildings and gracious mansions, but this is as nothing compared to frosty winter nights when the canal is covered with figures skating in the moonlight and the snowy slopes of the Gatineau Hills glitter as if scattered with diamonds. The canal ice is artificially thickened to make it safe by boring holes in it early in the season to allow water to well up from beneath and freeze on top.

OTTAWA

Key to map

1	Rideau Hall	10	Rideau Falls
2	City Hall	11	Royal Mint
3	Parliament Buildings	12	Canadian War Museum
4	Supreme Court	13	Canadian Ski Museum
5	Chateau Laurier Hotel	14	Major's Hill Park. Noon Gun
6	Tourist Bureau	15	Centennial Flame
7	Mackenzie King Bridge	16	Sparke Mall
8	Laurier Bridge	17	Byward Market
9	Ottawa University		

The restoration of buildings, villages and towns throughout the country is controlled by a foundation with its headquarters in Ottawa called Heritage Canada. There is a board of governors, eleven elected from the regions across the country. Founded in 1973 it is somewhat like the British National Trust, and gifts boost its regular income from an endowment fund. Although the movement is quite new in Canada it has already accomplished great things.

The parkway edging the Rideau Canal, is called the Queen Elizabeth Driveway and it makes a very pleasurable drive in the late spring when thousands of tulips are out. You can carry on for a further 2 miles (3 kilometres) through the Central Experimental Farm. This has an arboretum with over 1,000 trees and shrubs as part of its 1,200 acres (485 hectares) together with some herds of domestic animals. Strangers arriving in Ottawa along this route have been known to be confused, not believing when they see Jersey cows they are on the outskirts of the nation's capital.

Ottawa is fortunately well endowed with green open spaces. From Parliament Hill there is a view over the 54 acre (21 hectare) Hog's Back Park with attractive waterfalls; behind the Chateau Laurier in Majors Hill Park and the Rideau Canal with its flight of locks is just below another side of the hill. Perhaps the rural atmosphere enables politicians to take a less jaundiced view of their fellow men as they commute to work on skates in the winter.

6 MONTREAL AND FRENCH CANADA

Montreal is built partly on a plain and partly on natural terraces culminating in wooded Mount Royal, 886 feet (270 metres) high, from which it derives its name. The hill is surmounted by a cross which, if you fly in at night when it is illuminated, appears to be suspended in the sky. Founded by Maisonneuve in 1642, Montreal is a gateway to the interior of the North American continent with the St Lawrence Seaway system of canals connecting into the Great Lakes. It is understandable that the Indians resisted giving up such an enviable position.

During the eighteenth and nineteenth centuries under the French, Montreal prospered because of the demand in Europe for beaver pelts. When the British entered the scene they went out into the wilderness to trap and trade rather than wait, as had been done before, for the Indians to bring their wares to Montreal. The smaller fur-trading companies amalgamated in due course to join the North West Company which tried to compete with the Hudson's Bay Company. However, in 1821 these two giants joined forces and the Montreal base was given up in favour of St James Bay. This happened at the right time because the city was growing, other forms of commerce were coming to the fore and the port was full, due to its unique position in the New World. Its stability was even more assured when Montreal became the capital of Upper and Lower Canada by the 1841 Act of Union—a title which was lost to Kingston less than a decade later.

Today, Montreal is the largest metropolis in Canada and the second largest French-speaking one in the world after Paris itself. It can best be viewed from the north at the top of Mount Royal where a lacet roadway leads to the summit. If you have time it is traditional to do this in a horse-drawn carriage. You can gaze out to the east where Old Montreal lines the waterfront, there are residential areas and Olympic Park. To the west stretch the fashionable shopping malls and streets and the gracious houses of

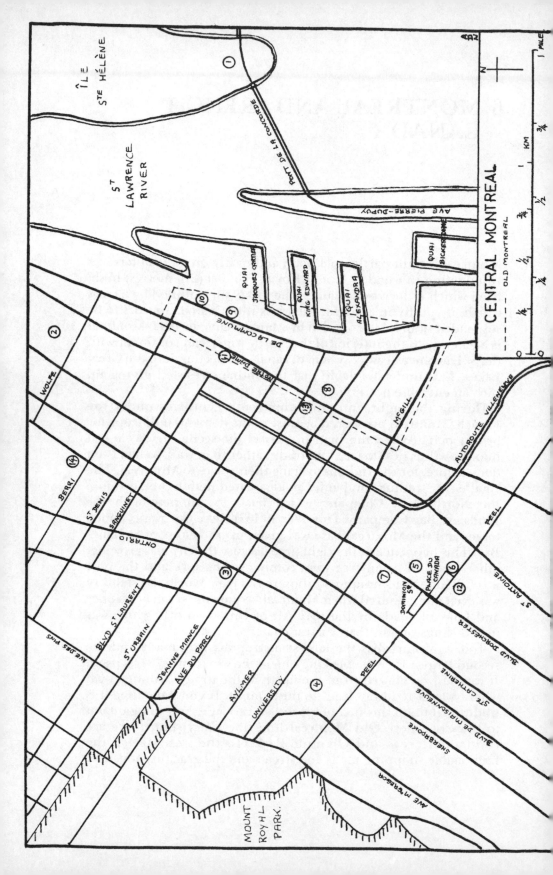

Westmount. Church spires and some of the taller new buildings help you to identify various sections and there are coin-operated telescopes if you do not have your binoculars with you. Here you are close to the Cross and also to St Joseph's Oratory, a Roman Catholic shrine.

The Cross was erected in 1924 as a reminder of a vow which Maisonneuve fulfilled in 1642. He promised to carry a cross on his shoulders to the summit in thanks to God if the flood, which threatened his small colony, receded. The infant city was spared and Maisonneuve planted his cross on the south slope. This was soon pulled down by the Iroquois and was replaced several times. The present steel cross weighs 26 tons and is 100 feet (30 metres) high. At night it is lit by 158 lightbulbs and is visible up to 30 miles (48 kilometres) when the weather is clear. It cost $25,000 and this was raised by schoolchildren through St Jean Baptiste Society.

Navigation is not a problem in Montreal as again it is laid out largely on a grid system. Make allowances for the French temperament which believe that speed and noise as well as skill are adjuncts to mobility. Turning right on a red light which is legal in Ontario, is forbidden in Quebec and the wearing of seatbelts is enforced. If, like many visitors, you choose to explore Old Montreal first, which is a compact area where walking is best, you will have time also to observe the local driving before plunging into it.

Organized walking tours, taking about an hour and a half, start from Place d'Armes which can easily be reached by the Metro. It is more fun to get a map and find your own way, perhaps stopping for lunch or dinner at one of the many good restaurants, or browsing in the antique shops. The tour takes you around what remains of a small walled city, and where places no longer exist

MONTREAL

Key to map

1	Man and his World	8	Notre Dame Cathedral
2	Maison du Radio Canada	9	Marche Bonsecours
3	Place des Arts	10	Notre Dame de Bonsecours
4	McGill University	11	Hotel de Ville de Montreal
5	Queen Elizabeth Hotel	12	Windsor Station
6	Chateau Champlain Hotel	13	Place d'Armes
7	Place Ville Marie	14	Voyageur Bus Station

there are plaques so that you can soon build up a picture of what old Montreal used to be like.

Of the buildings in this quarter two churches are outstanding for completely different reasons, one is large and the other very small. The first, the Gothic Cathedral of Notre Dame, has twin towers named Temperance and Perseverance which are 227 feet (69 metres) high and it is said resemble Westminster Abbey. James O'Donnell of New York was the architect. He was a Protestant but was converted to Roman Catholicism while it was being built and his grave is in the crypt. The west tower has a bell weighing over 12 tons. Although today it is electrically operated it is seldom used. The church holds a congregation of 5,000. The stained-glass windows are particularly interesting as they are not of religious scenes but of the colony in the early days.

The other church, tiny and the oldest in Montreal, is Notre-Dame-de-bon-secours built in 1657. It has been renovated several times and is referred to as the 'Sailor's Chapel'. It is most charming and unusual, reminiscent of some churches in Denmark, with model ships suspended from the ceiling carved by sailors in the past. The Madonna in the open steeple holds her arms out to the river. We were told that the appealing figure was carved by an artist who had come from Italy to enter a competition. The prize was quite a large sum of money—which he did not win. Then he realized he could not pay his fare home. He offered the Madonna to the church and he was given a ticket back to Italy.

Another statue erected in 1809 on a tall column is of none other than Lord Horatio Nelson. It is the oldest monument in Montreal and a forerunner of the one in Trafalgar Square. There is a building in the corner of Jacques Cartier Place, now a tobacconist shop, which used to be known as the 'Silver Dollar Saloon' because the owner had the floor inlaid with 350 silver dollars. At one time the City Hall also faced into Jacques Cartier Place. The Manoir Becancour next to it was for a time the residence of James McGill, founder of McGill University.

In the Place St Gabriel there is the historic Auberge Le Vieux St Gabriel's, a most interesting place to look around if you can take your eyes from the enticing menu for a few minutes. Another delightful place to eat is Les Filles du Roy, 415 Bonsecours, part of which extends into a glass conservatory full of lovely plants with an old wall outside. The sun gleams on a polished marble bar—the rest of the dining room also gleams but this time with well-polished old mahogany furniture. The background of this place is an interesting story.

Because few women came from France with the original traders, as villages and settlements grew and in order to increase the population of 'Nouvelle France', from 1663 to 1670 a movement was begun to attract young girls to cross the Atlantic. Louis XIV assured their dowries and one Marguerite Bourgenis, who founded the Bonsecours Chapel, took on the task of looking after them and instructing them in the art of housekeeping. One thousand girls crossed the sea to make new homes and many French Canadian families are descendants of 'Les Filles du Roy'.

There are numerous other buildings and places of interest in Old Montreal, for instance in the Place d'Armes there is a column with a statue on top of Maisonneuve, and north of this a classical building of the nineteenth century is the early Bank of Montreal. It has a museum inside. Should you lose your way in the labyrinth of narrow streets you can always pin-point your position by the high Nelson column.

There is really no better or more comfortable way of getting about Montreal than *Le Metro*. It has forty-three stations and needless to say many open into the bustling underground galleries which have more than 1,000 shops, cinemas, health clubs, banks and discos, not forgetting about sixty-five restaurants and bars. We watched a television show one afternon which was going out 'live' on one of the networks.

There are some 7 miles (11 kilometres) of subterranean galleries. Strange to think that while icy winds rage overhead and snow chokes roadways you can walk quite happily beneath it all without even wearing a coat. To people who do not experience such frigid conditions it may sound unhealthy to spend so much time in troglodytical fashion for part of each year. Yet it is easy to comprehend when you learn the startling fact that last winter Montreal spent 32 million dollars just to keep the city streets clear of snow. It can pile up over rooftops.

The Metro is the quietest so far built, for its spotlessly clean cars run on pneumatic wheels. One has heard of Moscow's underground stations with chandeliers but Montreal's Metro stations have been designed by individual architects and make you feel you are in an *Alice in Wonderland* kind of place with backlit stained-glass windows, sculptures and murals. One depicts the city fathers in the early days, another at the Place des Arts traces the history of music in Quebec. One wit has labelled the stations 'the world's largest underground art gallery'.

Up on the surface the Place des Arts is a most magnificent building which has facilities for ballet, opera, theatre and concerts. The large foyer with its red and grey panelling is decorated with shell designs, including the chandeliers.

Man and His World is an outdoor cultural centre on St Helen's Island in the St Lawrence River originally used for Expo' 67. Exhibitions are housed in the international pavilions which were built.

Although over 100 inches (255 centimetres) of snow floats down on the city each winter, the Montrealer can have the best of two worlds — and he does. While the underground galleries are useful for ignoring the snow, he can join the half million other Montrealers who rush to nearby parks to ski, skate or toboggan. The Olympic stadium's oval rink has room for 4,000 skaters and there are 278 smaller rinks to choose from together with snowshoeing areas and toboggan slides. There is even something new called the 'Snow Ball' which attracts tourists. You can stay for a couple of nights or a week in a choice of twenty-five Montreal hotels with daily transport to slopes within an hour's ride from the city centre and have dinner each evening at a further choice of fifteen restaurants. All-day lift tickets on the slopes are a bargain at about four dollars and ski clothing and gear can be rented if necessary. The 'Snow Ball' can be expensive or inexpensive — it depends on exactly what you want to do. The most central 'in town' park is Mount Royal itself which has two cross-country ski trails and an alpine ski-slope with lift, a toboggan run, an ice-skating rink on Beaver Lake, a large area for snowshoeing enthusiasts and winter picnic facilities.

One of the mountain landmarks is the Oratory of St Joseph, a place credited with miraculous powers like Lourdes in France. It was founded by a lay brother, St André, some fifty years ago and thousands of pilgrims visit it annually seeking cures. It is impressive to see the numerous crutches which have been left by cripples who no longer needed them. Not all penitents who visit the shrine are invalids and St André himself might be amused at the Newfoundland story I was told about one such man. You can seek forgiveness by going up steps to the oratory on your knees. An elderly lady was having difficulty with a rather voluminous dress and, looking behind, asked a young man if he would help lift her skirt. 'No, I'm afraid not,' he replied. 'It is for doing that, that I am doing this.'

Overlooked by Mount Royal, Place Ville Marie has elegant shops and hotels, its outstanding building being the forty-two-storey high Royal Bank Office Tower. Sherbrooke Street is a shopper's paradise with many exclusive boutiques and St Catherine Street is one of the longest thoroughfares in the country with all the well-known store chains represented. Montrealers are renowned for their fashion flair. Everywhere there are restaurants and cafés. South of St Catherine Street, at Peel Street, Dominion Square is the heart of the downtown business section where many sightseeing tours begin. A park for many years, Dominion Square has several monuments including a statue of the Scottish poet, Robert Burns, erected by local admirers in 1930 and one to commemorate the Canadians killed during the Boer War. The square is bordered by the Canadian Imperial Bank of Commerce building, the Sun Life and Dominion Square building and one of Montreal's long-established hotels, the Windsor. Next comes Place du Canada which is surrounded by Mary Queen of the World Cathedral, the Archbishop's Palace, St George's Anglican Church, Windsor station and the Chateau Champlain Hotel. The latter has several excellent restaurants and unusual eyebrow-shaped windows. The Queen Elizabeth Hotel is close by, its main restaurant nudging the sky twenty-one storeys up, its Beaver Club recapturing early fur-trading days with its woodland murals.

Montreal is headquarters for Canadian Pacific and Canadian National Railways and Air Canada. Its new international airport, Mirabel, is vast when compared with the older Dorval and has the latest innovations for speeding passengers and their luggage on their way quickly. The place is never crowded, even car parking is no problem if you are in a tearing hurry. One big disadvantage however is that from Mirabel it takes a good hour to drive the 34 miles (55 kilometres) into Montreal whereas Dorval is less than half an hour away being only 13 miles (21 kilometres) from the centre of the city.

Thinking of distances the Montrealers are fortunate in having the Laurentian Mountains close by and many have summer cottages along the lakes. You go via the high-speed Laurentian Autoroute (toll 25 cents every 25 miles) and Highway 117 which passes through many of the major resort places. In winter the roads are kept open and there is the new 'Ski train' idea called Petit Train du Nord which is run by Canadian Pacific at weekends. Skiers can leave the train at various stations and ski across country more or less following the line of the railway so that, when they have had enough, they go to the next station and board the train returning to Montreal. Packed picnics can be taken along or ordered in the train and some skiers prefer station meals. Food is cooked with care in the Laurentians for each restaurant has its own colourful chef and for some reason, although he is often tempted by the offer of higher wages to go and cook in one of the city hotels or restaurants, it is usually impossible to woo him away.

You will have gathered that from this there is a high standard of cuisine not always found elsewhere and it should not surprise you to see on the menu such things as langouste cardinal or breast of capon in vin rosé perhaps with truffles or goose liver. You should also leave room for crêpes suzettes, baked Alaska or 'delices des Rois'—miniature ice-cream puffs bursting with smooth vanilla ice cream afloat in chocolate sauce with Grand Marnier poured over them.

The little mountain towns and villages are reminiscent of Switzerland. Some of the houses have the appearance of chalets, with gently sloping roofs in 'cloche' form. The lower edge, called the 'weeper' curves slightly outwards especially at the front to protect the walls from falling snow. Sometimes the front roofing protrudes so far it has to be supported with wooden pillars, these in turn are often enclosed by a low balustrade.

The village of St Jerome acts as one of the gateways to the mountains. It was founded in 1830 by a legendary priest, Curé Labelle, who went on foot and by canoe into the country to select sites for new parishes. He was responsible for some twenty in all and invited French, Swiss and Belgians to come and 'colonize' the new land. He stood six feet (1.82 metres) tall and is said to have tipped the scales at 333 pounds (151 kilos). This must have been a slight exaggeration but it proves that he more than enjoyed the good Laurentian fare.

Mont Tremblant Park was established in 1894 by the Quebec Government. It is a vast territory controlled by the Province, designed to provide the people of Quebec and visitors with an outdoor leisure place of exceptional beauty. It has many ski centres, resorts and a fish hatchery at Saint-Fauston. The reason for its name is again connected with good food. After hunting in the district, several Indians enjoyed a hearty meal and lay under the shelter of some trees to sleep it off. The thunder of a nearby waterfall made them think, while half asleep, that the earth itself was trembling.

Val David is a year-round tourist and sports resort at an altitude of 1,056 feet (322 metres). Many artists live there and craftsmen produce copper enamelling, engravings, pottery, jewellery and rustic furniture. For children there is the nearby Santa Claus Village open from May to December. Val David is about 50 miles (80 kilometres) north of Montreal and its deluxe hotel, La Sapinière, has sixty-seven rooms, a swimming pool, overlooks a most lovely lake and the meals are exquisite, so much so that it is the only Canadian hotel mentioned in the international Relais de Campagne. The Quebec Ministry of Tourism has awarded it five fleurs de lys for its comfortably appointed rooms and four forks (the maximum) for the quality of its cuisine. The chef, Marcel Kretz, born in Strasbourg, has many awards and generously gave me several of his delicious recipes for the chapter in this book on food and drink. The hotel wine cellar can be visited; sometimes small dinners are given in part of it and there are some 200 different brands and vintages.

Here is a specimen menu served at La Sapinière recently to some businessmen. The note explains the omission of soup.

Note: No consommé or soup is served on this menu, because the special entrée 'Wild Mushrooms' should have the full benefit of the 'surprise', which is a puff pastry cover which will rise under the effect of the steaming wild mushrooms (boletus, meadow mushroom, chanterelles, lactarius)

Laurentian Wild Mushrooms 'en surprise'
Quenelles of Pike, lobster sauce
Roast Boneless and Stuffed Rack of Canadian Lamb
'Culinary Olympics Frankfurt 1976'
Oyster Plant, Meunière
Buttered Mauve Broccoli
Croquette Potatoes with Sesame Seeds
Watercress Salad
Cheese Tray
Strawberry Coupe Andalouse
Petits Fours
Mokka

Grey Rocks Inn close to the village of St Jovite is the doyen of the Laurentian Mountain resorts and was well known before the Second World War. Its ski season begins in late November and lasts until mid-April. Many of the forty instructors have known the slopes for the last decade or more. They start beginners off by a method called 'Short Ski Progression' using short skis designed for easy stopping and turning which gives assurance within hours rather than days. Grey Rocks has been a pioneer in sports, starting skiing in the early thirties and having its first tennis court as long ago as 1910. Once the snow melts and summer comes then tennis begins and of course fishing and swimming. If by nightfall you have a little surplus energy to spare, there is dancing and of course in the Laurentians the best meal of the day — dinner.

It is always fun to do something different for the first time and we decided to go from Montreal to Quebec by the Voyageur Bus. They offer a special service on this route, the vehicle being equipped and operated along aircraft lines. You pay a fare supplement and for this you get a limited number of passengers, a meal served to you in your seat and room to get up and move about. There is even a radio telephone service and the journey is shorter than the ordinary buses. We looked forward to sitting comfortably and enjoying the country through which we passed and reported to the bus terminal at the appointed hour only to be told that there was a 24-hour strike, so we had to go by train instead and this proved to be a less than exhilarating experience.

We had looked forward to an upmarket service between the two cities some 150 miles (240 kilometres) apart. In the event it was a single diesel railcar which stopped at every small halt and finally arrived at Quebec station, some 7 miles (11 kilometres) out of the city, after midnight. It cost us nearly as much to get a taxi into Quebec as the rail journey itself but the welcome at La Concorde Hotel more than made up for our low spirits.

Having been shown to our room and unpacked we suddenly thought longingly of that dinner we should have had on the bus. Remembering that in similar circumstances elsewhere we had only been able to get a sandwich and cup of coffee we wondered if we should just go to bed and the next day break a long standing custom of our marriage by having a really out-of-this-world breakfast. My spouse was hungry and suggested that I telephone, adding that a female voice might be more appealing if indeed a waiter was still on duty. I picked up the receiver and a lively voice assured me that the coffee shop was not closed and we could have anything on the menu. What a welcome this was in Quebec. Our waiter could not have been more attentive and I do not remember when a hot toasted turkey sandwich and glass of cold lager tasted so heavenly.

Gazing up at Quebec from the St Lawrence river, on its high rocky promontory burrowing into the steep cliff face on two levels, it might be as impregnable as a crusader fortress. Again, with its grey stone walls, martello towers and stone buildings crowned by the Chateau Frontenac, its jade-green turrets up in the clouds, it might equally be a fortified Ruritanian city. Actually the Chateau Frontenac is the most famous of the CPR hotels, the impregnable walls had their gates removed as long ago as 1871 at the same time as the ramparts were lowered to chest level and in modern parlance Quebec is often referred to as the 'Split level City'. Nevertheless it has the honour of being the only walled city in Canada and if Cartier and Champlain could see what their foundling has grown into today, they would be as fascinated as the visitor.

Like the Concorde aircraft, the latter-day product of English and French co-operation, Quebec too shares the styles of both nations. The French started the walls between the Cap aux Diamant and the Cote du Palais while British engineers completed them to the Chateau Saint Louis. The Chateau Frontenac Hotel too is an Anglo-French affair which is part of its charm. When the great city gates were removed by the French due to the persuasion of Lord Dufferin the Governor General, the walls remained to beautify the city. The terrace, 200 feet (60 metres) above the river, was named after him. Just above it is a memorial in the form of a plinth to Wolfe and Montcalm with this inscription: 'Valour gave them a common death, history a common fame, posterity a common monument.'

It is difficult to decide whether to visit the Upper or the Lower town first. To get to the lower part you can either drive down, walk down a long flight of steps known as the 'Breakneck' Stairs or for 25 cents travel down by the *ascenseur*, a cog-wheel operated lift said to be the oldest in Canada but still sturdy. If you wish to take this only one way it is better to use it going up as walking to the upper level is quite a climb. You will find yourself in the market place of old Quebec, Place Royale, just as it was originally. The façades, doorways and old shop fronts have been restored. Most delightful of all, many of the houses have been turned into museums so that you can visit them and see the authentic furniture of the first French settlers.

The Church of Our Lady of Victories is the focal point of the square, its name attributed to the destruction of English ships threatening the city in 1711 and Frontenac's victory in 1690. The altar is significant, being built in the form of a fort complete with loopholes and turrets, said to be like the one destroyed by Wolfe's forces. A seventeenth-century beautifully carved model ship hangs from the ceiling. It is believed that on the site of this church

Champlain put up his first living quarters, a stockade, store and garden. As well as the charming houses, leave a little spare time to visit the Maison des Vins in the Fornel house across the square. Although it is actually a provincial liquor store where you can shop, it certainly is one with a difference. The interior is dimly lit and bottles line the grey stone walls. Vintage wines and brandies are displayed in glass cabinets, their background, suitably enough, being champagne corks. As you go further in you descend four steps into a vaulted cellar, complete with wine and beer casks. It is even darker and although cobwebs do not brush your face nor is the smell of dust evident, you get that intangible atmosphere of a French *cave*. The Quebecois treat wine with the respect it deserves.

Opposite Sous-le-Fort Street where Recoller priests built their first chapel in 1615, there is the house of Louis Jolliet who was born in Quebec, studied at the Jesuit college to be a priest but eventually went into the fur trade. Together with Father Maquette he discovered the Mississippi river in 1674. You go through his house which acts as an entrance to the *ascenseur* which will return you to Dufferin Terrace.

Before you leave the lower town however, if there is time to spare, you must not miss seeing the replica of the little ship 'La Grande Hermine' in which Jacques Cartier wintered in 1535. It is moored in the St Charles river basin. She spent her first summer afloat at the site of Expo '67 in Montreal.

The Tourist and Convention Department of the Quebec Urban Community at 60 Rue d'Auteuil, just inside the St Louis Gate will give you a most comprehensive little free booklet called *Walking Tour of Old Quebec* which is in English and French. It not only gives you the history and details of all the places you may visit but is delightful to keep as a souvenir.

Back in the upper town, when you get out of the elevator to your right is Montmorency Park, named after the first bishop of Quebec François de Montmorency-Laval—who also gave his name to Laval University. Cartier's statue is in the middle of the park. He wears a long frock coat and, with right foot forward and right hand extended, looks as though he is about to come and greet you. If you turn to the left along Dufferin Terrace you will walk into an extension called Promenade des Gouverneurs and continue beneath the walls of the star-shaped Citadel built by the British on top of old French fortifications. The Citadel can also be reached from Place d'Armes, about a ten minute walk. If you wish to enter there is a small fee and you can see ancient guns, ramparts, towers, barracks and go over a military museum. In the summer the Royal 22nd Regiment changes guard at 10 a.m. Beyond the Citadel you come to the Plains of Abraham and Battlefield Park, where the Wolfe-Montcalm encounter which had such repercussions, was decided within half an hour. Here you can see two martello towers built between 1804-6 and monuments and plaques describing the battle. Also in the park you can see the spot at which King George VI, the first reigning British monarch to visit the Dominion accompanied by Queen Elizabeth, first set foot on Canadian soil on 17 May 1939.

Rising high above Quebec's dramatic cliffs and Dufferin Terrace in Place d'Armes overlooking the majestic St Lawrence river, is the city's renowned building—the Chateau Frontenac. Inserted in its outer walls are plaques recalling historic events. Over the archway entrance is the crest of Governor Montmagny who succeeded Quebec's founder Samuel de Champlain. He was a knight of the most Venerable Order of the Hospital of St John of Jerusalem and beneath it, scarcely readable, are the words 'Stone carved for the Priory of the Knights of Malta, Quebec, 1647.' The Governor had hoped that a Priory of this order would be set up in Quebec.

The Frontenac crest is above the courtyard entrance facing Place d'Armes. It is a blue shield with three golden griffin paws, above which a coronet has golden spikes tipped with pearls. Another plaque states that:

'Here stood the Chateau Haldimand, or Vieux Chateau, occupying part of the outworks of the Fort St. Louis. Begun in 1784, completed in 1787, this edifice was displaced by the erection of the present Chateau Frontenac in 1892.'

Immediately opposite it another plaque honours the officers and men of the 7th regiment of Fusiliers who defended the city in 1775 and 1776. In January 1947 a further plaque was added in commemoration of the Allied leaders who met there for two conferences during the Second World War.

At the beginning of the hotel project the Chateau Frontenac Company was fortunate to have President Van Horne of the CPR at the helm as was the case with Banff Springs and, probably due to his foresight, the architect was again Bruce Price who was made responsible for the structural design and exterior. Elegance and convenience, luxury and simplicity; ancient without, modern within, these were the guiding principles that governed the building of the Chateau Frontenac.

At the time the original building was erected in 1892-3, and for many years thereafter until the building was completed as it now stands, the furniture of the Chateau Frontenac was chosen with minutest care. When the tower suites were being furnished in 1924, the firm of architects, Edward and W. S. Maxwell of Montreal, who had designed the tower to accord with Bruce Price's original building, sent a special commissioner to England and France, at the behest of the Canadian Pacific Railway Company, in search of genuine antiques, and to make arrangements for the finest of copies to be made of such originals as were not for sale. On this mission Mr Edward Maxwell visited seventeen cathedral towns in England and almost as many in France. While in Paris he dealt with a firm which was, at that time, the only one in France allowed to remove pieces from the National Museums for reproduction purposes.

At the foot of the first Grand Staircase there was a statue of General James Wolfe, now removed to the Chateau Halifax. It is by the well-known Canadian sculptor, Dr Tait McKenzie. The Jacques Cartier room overlooking Place d'Armes square is quite unique, its theme being a representation, as nearly as possible, of the interior of the cabin of Jacques Cartier on his ship 'La Grande Hermine.'

The Champlain Room is a long and restful lounge, overlooking the terrace, with the largest fireplace in the Chateau. The gold and blue ballroom is said to be a replica of the Hall of Mirrors at Versailles, with the exception of windows instead of mirrors and the appointments are in Louis XV style.

The Chateau Frontenac's predecessor, the Chateau St Louis, was nearly burned down in January 1834 and, by a strange coincidence, in the same month of the year but over a century later in 1926 the hotel almost met a similar fate. Fire broke out about dusk in the Riverside Wing on a bitterly cold day and similar to that other January day. In the wintry conditions water froze as it was played onto the building but fortunately it was possible to contain the fire and the damage though bad enough could have been much worse. Nobody was injured, most of the furniture, tapestries and paintings came through unscathed and restoration was accomplished in 127 working days by a force of 1,200 men.

Today the Chateau Frontenac has 550 rooms, twenty suites and four restaurants. It is welcoming with a personality of its own. The views over the river are spectacular and as always it offers everything up to the minute but still retains its old-world charm, including its delectable French Canadian cuisine, salmon from Gaspé, beef from Calgary—even frogs' legs from France.

Quebec has a winter carnival in early February for ten days when, however cold and icy the weather, everyone has a good time. Despite ice floes there is a thrilling canoe race across the St Lawrence, ice hockey games, bonfires and fireworks, winter sports are continuous except when there is a parade. Snowmen and other sculptured snow figures stand in front of houses and line streets. I have said that nobody notices the cold but *caribou* may have a little to do with that, so be warned. The merry makers rush around warmly clad and brandishing hollow plastic canes and that's where the *caribou* comes in—it's a mixture of spirits and red wine!

Beyond the city walls Quebec spreads out in all directions; there are churches, Laval University, hotels like the high rise Hilton, shopping centres, parks and avenues of attractive boutiques and antique shops. The most enjoyable way, while on holiday, is to hire a horse-drawn *calèche* to explore the narrow streets. You will find a row of them awaiting you in Place d'Armes. Nearby on the Terrace is a statue of Champlain, feathered hat in hand looking debonair with cloak swinging out from his shoulders. Quebec's environs are interesting too, particularly some 18 miles (29 kilometres) north-west where there are the Montmorency Falls, higher than Niagara but not in the same impressive setting, and the Basilica of Saint Anne de Beaupré a famous shrine like that of St Joseph's Oratory in Montreal. Thousands of pilgrims come here every year to seek cures for their illness and in the same way as in Montreal, you cannot but be impressed by the hundreds of crutches that have been left behind by those with sufficient faith to have been healed.

It is always encouraging to hear of someone miraculously cured when there seems to be no hope. My one story of the Basilica occurred several years ago when I did not know that I should ever see it. A friend of ours, who had been in the 8th Army during the last war, was in the retreats and advances in the western desert. At one time when the British were falling back and had to disperse, he and a few comrades lost their way. They were finally rescued by some monks who took them to their small monastery and cared for them for several days. Later they rejoined their unit but the incident was not forgotten. Several years later our friend remembered the kindly monks and, living in Ireland at the time, ordered an embroidered altar cloth from a convent. It was duly delivered to him and he sent it to the monastery. Several months passed and one day he received a parcel which was a gift of thanks for his altar cloth in the form of a golden crucifix studded with gems. He was quite overcome by the magnificence of this gift and, when he later moved to Canada and settled near Quebec, presented it to the Basilica Saint Anne de Beaupré. They were delighted to have such a treasure to add to their collection and, as a result, the little girls belonging to our friend were educated in the convent.

7 NEW BRUNSWICK AND PRINCE EDWARD ISLAND

We were told by friends in Victoria that the only city in the country to compare with theirs for sheer beauty is Fredericton which is the capital of New Brunswick, the largest of the Maritime Provinces. It is certainly a beautiful place and we could not have visited it at a better time for it was in autumn when the maple leaves had turned shades of scarlet, purple and yellow.

Fredericton is built along the quiet reaches of the Saint John River and has absorbed so much of its serene and scenic charm that it is sometimes called the 'City of Stately Elms'. These tall trees often meet overhead in avenues where families enjoy the mellowing houses and gardens of their ancestors. Lawns and flower beds edge verandahs on which people sit during summer evenings before strolling to The Green where they meet friends or watch the sunset's reflections on the water. 'The Green' is the name given to the parkland lining the river's edge where willows bend to the water. At this time of year in sun-dappled shade across from the river are some of the city's most charming buildings, including the Cathedral. As with so many Canadian towers and turrets, the steeple and roofing, due to the weathering of the copper sheathing, have a pale patina of jade green.

Christ Church Cathedral is said to be the first to have been built on British soil after the Norman Conquest in 1066. It is in Gothic style and the clock in its slender tower was designed by Lord Grimthorpe and predates London's Big Ben. It even has a ghost—a nurse trained by no less a person than Florence Nightingale. She married the first bishop, John Medley and her apparition has been seen hurrying across the lawn and into the church by the west door.

Further along on the same side of the street is the Legislative Assembly Building. It is in Corinthian style with a 135 foot (40 metres) high dome. Its entrance is through a portico lined with pillars. Once through the vestibule you find yourself in an octagonal hallway at the end of which a spiral staircase leads to higher storeys. There is no entrance fee and, when the house is in session, you may watch from the public gallery if there is room. The Assembly Chamber is not large but has a very high ceiling rising some 40 feet (12 metres) up through two floors of the building. On either side of the throne there are two paintings by Sir Joshua Reynolds of King George III and Queen Charlotte. New Brunswick was named after the King's ancestral seat, Brunswick in Germany. Above the throne hang the colours of the Carleton and York Regiment.

The library contains some 45,000 books, its two greatest treasures being a copy of the Domesday Book and a rare four-volume set of Audubon bird books more than 3 feet (1 metre) high, containing hand-coloured engravings and bought in 1853. One of the most beautiful plates is of a pine finch drawn by Audubon in the grounds of Government House in 1832.

Across Queen Street from the Legislative Assembly Building is the Beaverbrook Gallery, one of his many gifts to the city and a great tourist attraction. It is dominated by the great Santiago el Grande by the Spanish surrealist, Salvador Dali. In the British section are works by Sir Joshua Reynolds, Thomas Gainsborough, Constable, Romney, Turner and Hogarth. Among the modern artists are Graham Sutherland and Walter Richard Sickert, plus four canvases by Winston Churchill. There are several by the Group of Seven and some thirty works by Cornelius Kreighoff. One of the latter's paintings called 'Merrymaking' shows a Breughel the Elder influence. Kreighoff is the best know of the Canadian 'primitives'. This small gallery is one of the most outstanding in Canada. 'The Beaver's' remark was apt when he said that the most beautiful picture was looking through a window at the gently flowing Saint John River. He loved Fredericton and across from the art gallery is another of his gifts, the Playhouse Theatre.

In a park adjoining the hotel called, you have guessed it, the Beaverbrook, there is a statue of him and at his feet a family of bronze beavers frolic in a fountain. Not content with his benificence, he endowed Fredericton University with buildings and scholarships. Although Fredericton was his great love, he was born Max Aitken, son of the local Presbyterian minister in the small town of Newcastle. His climb up the ladder of success was heartily applauded by the townsfolk. As a youngster he had been a newspaper delivery boy, a fact he found amusing when he became a press baron. When he was elevated to the peerage for his work in

England, he chose the name of Beaverbrook as, when young, his great joy was to fish in a stream where beavers built their intricate homes. In recognition of his achievements Newcastle presented its town square to him whereupon he embellished it by sending seventeenth-century garden seats from Syon Park House in Middlesex, England and a wrought iron gazebo from Italy. When he died his ashes were placed at the base of his monument in Newcastle.

Fredericton was a garrison town in the old days and many retired officers lived there so it is not surprising that, when Empire loyalists arrived from the United States in increasing numbers, they too were drawn to the town. Their coming enhanced the atmosphere of stability and unchanging life which is still evident. Life continues at a leisurely pace and family traditions linger on. I have not seen it but I have been told about the gravestone in one of the churchyards which relates that a gentleman at the age of ninety two 'turned to God and thereafter lived a good life'. However, life in Fredericton is far from being dull routine and there have been unique happenings. One such is the saga of the Coleman frog which calls for some explanation.

The Military Compound is now a federal historic site and includes the guard house, officers' quarters and enlisted men's barracks. The York-Sunbury Historical museum is housed in the officers' quarters and here you can not only see authentic furnishings of the nineteenth century but the Coleman frog in a large glass case. He was a young but gigantic frog weighing about 7 pounds (3 kilos) when Fred Coleman first saw him. The following weekend Fred took his cronies along on a fishing trip to see the frog. He was no figment of the imagination and the men fed him with Junebugs, buttermilk and, it is said, rye whiskey. Each weekend the frog waited for his human friends and the strange human food they brought him. He grew and grew.

One weekend when Fred went fishing his froggy friend was still there—but dead. He took the body to a taxidermist and for nearly half a century the frog sat in the lobby of Fred's hotel in a huge glass case. No child felt he really knew Fredericton without a visit to see the Coleman frog and finally it was decided that it should be moved to the museum where you can see it today. Because Fredericton is such a down-to-earth place, some visitors think the frog may be a papier maché model. However, we were fortunate in that we did not have to decide if it was real or not because our charming guide around Fredericton was Helen-Jean Newman and it was her great-uncle Fred Coleman who found the frog.

From Fredericton, 23 miles (37 kilometres) to the west lies Kings Landing Historical Settlement. Here you really go back in time for at least a century because over fifty buildings on 300 acres (120 hectares) step back to the period 1790-1870 and include a general store, blacksmith's shop, and a working sawmill. During the summer, costumed guides, some living in the buildings, portray a vivid picture of early pioneer life and lend authenticity. They have gone to great trouble to convince themselves and the visitor that they are actually living the life of two centuries ago. The general store contains the things which it would have done in those days. There is the frame house of an ex-army major who is supposed to own the sawmill and be justice of the peace. The village cobbler assists at the King's Head Inn at night. The mill operates at various times and the 'employees' will explain how it works. Oxen wait patiently while farm labourers load wagons with hay. You will not find any radios, TV, cars, tractors or refrigerators. Instead housewives visit Fred Perley's store to buy the food which they will cook using the recipes of that period. Part of the charm for the visitor is the smell of freshly baked bread, roasting game or meat on a spit or molasses cookies being removed from a stove oven.

The King's Head Inn is a fine place to eat. The building was a hotel in the 1920s and became a private home again a few years later. It was among the houses moved to Kings Landing and has been restored as a typical wayside coaching inn of the mid 1850s with period decor, furnishings and refreshments. Here is the weekly bill of fare:

Day by Day Specials
Soup or Cider, Coffee, Tea or Milk
Monday
Mrs Long's Chicken Vegetable Pie with Creamed Potatoes
Tuesday
George III Roast Beef with Baked Potato and Carrots
Wednesday
Parson's Preference—Hot Meat Pie with Creamed Potatoes
Thursday
Captain Jones' Baked Ham with Scalloped Potatoes and Cauliflower in Cream Sauce
Friday
Riverman's Joy—Baked Fillet of Fish with Mashed Potatoes and a Vegetable

OR Seafood Chowder with Hot Rolls
Saturday
Governor Carleton Baked Beans and Brown Bread
OR Dubliner's Delight—Beef Braised in Guiness with Creamed
Potatoes and Vegetables
OR Seafood Chowder and Hot Rolls
Sunday
Squire Ingraham's Crackling Roast Pork with Mashed Potatoes
Turnip, Dressing and Apple Sauce
OR Seafood Chowder and Hot Rolls

The Reverend Ted Eaton is vicar of St Mark's Church in Kings Landing and served in New Brunswick parishes for nine years before becoming a worker-priest and Information Officer there. He has an avid interest in early history and is a writer and radio commentator—when he has time from looking after his flock and showing people round. An unusual idea which is working well at Kings Landing is that children can go there on holiday, enter the life of the place, dress the part and play with the children who stay there all summer. They particularly enjoy the dressing up and helping with the farm animals and pets.

An Acadian village near Caraquet is run on the same lines as Kings Landing. It required seven years of research and construction. Today you can see life there as it would have been in an Acadian settlement during the period from 1780 to 1880. In those days life was harsh for there were few material possessions following the Acadian expulsion of 1755, and this village is run along austere lines.

The province has many unique attractions but one of particular delight to visitors of all ages, especially if they have cameras, are the 'covered' or 'kissing' bridges. You also get these in Nova Scotia but in New Brunswick they are claimed to be longer. This is certainly true at Hartland, about 75 miles (120 kilometres) north of Fredericton where one is 1,282 feet (390 metres) long. Apart from local traffic it is not used much these days because the heavy vehicles take advantage of a new modern structure a bit further up river. The old bridge is remarkable and you can almost hear the clippety-clop of horses' hooves and imagine the kissing of courting couples in the dark. These covered bridges were made to protect the actual bridge from snow and there are over a hundred in New Brunswick. The entrance has a black, pointed roof and the sides are timber, usually painted red. The first time I saw one it reminded me of the 'little red schoolhouse' of children's stories. I must confess I have heard them described as an 'elongated cowshed' but only the unpoetic would think that.

I had never eaten fiddlehead until I came to New Brunswick. It is delicious, the taste not unlike delicate, thin steamed asparagus. In the same way as the Indians discovered wild rice, they found the fiddlehead and, like most superb delicacies, it only has a short season and that in the early spring. They should be served hot, drenched with butter and are perhaps at their best served with salmon. Fiddleheads are gathered along river banks and are of the fern family. They have to be picked while the stem and head are 'full of goodness' and although you can sometimes buy them frozen from the supermarket, nothing quite tastes like a tender fiddlehead freshly plucked! Its name originated through resemblance to the fiddle but of course fiddleheads were growing in the wilds long before violins were invented. The traditional way to cook them is in boiling water with a sprinkling of salt, the same way you would do baby new potatoes and they can be a separate course in themselves.

If you are offered a purple vegetable in a restaurant it may not be broccoli but could be dulse, a dried seaweed. It is not an Indian dish this time but one first appreciated in Scotland. People in New Brunswick love it and it is easily obtained as it flourishes in the Bay of Fundy. When the tide is low it is gathered up by the basketful. Residents living near Saint John can pick their own from the seashore and like most vegetables, when fresh it is at its best. People living inland buy it from greengrocers or supermarkets. It has a salty tang and I must confess I do not like it. However, it is good for you and full of iodine. You can buy it in dry powder form and add it to casseroles and other dishes for seasoning.

Motoring in New Brunswick is always a pleasure because much of it is alongside lakes or the Saint John River. You will not go far through a forest or over a hill without catching a tantalizing glimpse of water. Driving along the famous Blue Ridge Mountain highway in Virginia, which is such a spectacular route, I could not think why I was not greatly impressed. Suddenly it came to me that it was because there was no water—no rivers, waterfalls or lakes.

Wherever we go we always enjoy finding unusual signs. We saw many in Canada: 'Beware of Falling Rock' seemed self explanatory until we were told a story. A beautiful Indian maiden had two suitors, Flowing Stream and Falling Rock. She finally married the former and Falling Rock is still planning to scalp his rival. Hence the sign! My husband always derides the slippery road sign maintaining that no car could make such skid marks unless it crossed its legs. We try to photograph these signs where possible but did not have a camera handy for one on the ticket office at Crabbe Mountain which read— 'Frostbite danger today is mild.'

Route 102 takes you from Fredericton to Saint John (when referring to the town the Saint is never abbreviated) some 70 miles (112 kilometres) distant and you drive through some of the loveliest countryside in the province. On the way at Oromocto, a large military base, an 1871 blockhouse, Fort Hughes, has been reconstructed on the river bank. Small ferries ply back and forth across the river at various points. They are free and give you a break from driving and a chance to enjoy the scenery or indeed visit the other bank. The river mouth was discovered by Champlain on St John the Baptist's Day in 1604 so he named it after the saint.

At Gagetown, Queens County Museum was formerly the home of Sir Leonard Tilley, one of the Fathers of Confederation. You can buy handwoven cloth and various things at Loomcrofters, a company which uses as its store a two-hundred-year-old blockhouse.

The Saint John tourist bureau near King Square will give you a map called 'The Loyalist Trail' which takes you on an hour's walk around the interesting parts of the city. Even if you do not have an hour to spare, their first suggestion is one of the most interesting and just next door. It is the local Court House built in 1828 with the most surprising spiral staircase which attracts hundreds of tourists. More than one hundred tons of stone was quarried in Scotland to make it. Edged by a handsome wrought-iron railing, one assumes that each slab has a large portion embedded in the wall to hold it. However, this is not so and the structure is perfectly balanced and largely self-supporting.

From the Court House turn left and around the corner to King Street past the town gaol. No prisoner could ever escape through the back wall however deep a tunnel as it is part of a hillside. You now come to something that every schoolchild has heard about and that is 'the little red schoolhouse'. It was built in the Queens County community of Bella Vista and was presented to the city during Canada's centennial.

It is very strange to English eyes to see how they move houses in Canada. With our brick construction of course it is impossible, but the ordinary Canadian house is of timber placed on top of a half-buried concrete basement. It can be jacked up on to a special trailer and towed to a new destination and this is quite commonly done. We asked the tractor driver of one such rig in Quebec, who was getting petrol at the same garage, what was happening. He told us that someone had been left the house in a will and, rather than move from his home town to live in it, he was having it brought to him. The move includes men sitting on the house roof to disconnect power and telephone lines while the load passes.

Another Centennial gift is The Old General Store museum presented by the Barbour Company, who were spice merchants in the old days. This was moved in a different manner to the house we saw in Quebec for it was floated some 80 miles (130 kilometres) down river from Sheffield. Today it is stocked with authentic old merchandise. Entrance is free as is the dulse if the tide has just been out, and it can be tasted at no cost so that the tourist can make up his mind whether he likes it or not. There is an old-time barber shop at the back and, though you cannot have your hair cut or hear a barber shop quartette, you can admire the iron chairs and the rows of scented pomades. If you have a moustache you may find your fingers whirling the ends and almost reaching for the wax.

The pathways in King Square are laid out to represent the original Union Flag used by the Loyalists before the Union Jack came into being. In one corner of the square there is a large oddly shaped piece of metal. No, it is not a bronze by Henry Moore or a meteorite or even a hunk of Skylab, it is a great mass of metal objects and heaven-knows-what, discovered in the debris of a burned-down store in 1837 when over one hundred buildings were razed to the ground in a devastating fire.

Despite the fire one charming old mansion remains at the corner of Germain and Union streets. This Georgian-type home, called The Loyalist House, is open to the public from June to September. It has twin flights of steps leading to the front door which has an Adam-shaped fanlight above it. Inside the main hall there is an attractive curving staircase and the rooms have period furniture.

The New Brunswick Museum with its lovely pediment above its pillared façade is actually Canada's oldest—built in 1842. All kinds of interesting things are on display from an innocent collection of dolls to a menacing figurehead of the 'Queen of Hearts', a locally built ship fated to have a man killed on every voyage she made. There is also a fine collection of ship models. The museum is open daily in the summer from 10 a.m. to 9 p.m., admission 50 cents.

Across from King Square there is an ancient burial ground with headstones dating back to the 1700s and close by you can visit the Old City Market which has been in use for the last century. Here you can get fresh vegetables, fruit and meat, also baskets and other handwoven things made by the Indians.

Perhaps the greatest attraction outside the town is that of the Reversing Falls, a dramatic sight where a series of rapids and whirlpools rushing back and forth are caused by the flow of the river colliding with that of the tide.

Moncton is 88 miles (140 kilometres) north-east of Saint John and nestles along the Petitcodiac river. On the way you go through Sackville, a town whose population is only 3,000, yet it is Canada's international shortwave broadcasting station and the Canadian Broadcasting Corporation's Maritime Transmitter CBA. It has a religious theme for here was the site of the first Baptist, Methodist and Roman Catholic churches in Canada and nearby is the historic Fort Beausejour.

Mount Allison University in this pleasant unpretentious town is well known and was founded by Charles Frederick Allison in 1840. The campus has splendid buildings, green lawns with fountains, lily ponds and tree-lined avenues. There are over 1,200 students.

Once you reach Moncton you can easily find Main Street and there watch another phenomenon, known as the Tidal Bore. Like that in the river Severn in England and those in other parts of the world, it is caused by the incoming tide rushing into the funnel-shaped inlet where the river meets the sea. As this narrows it concentrates the advancing sea water which moves upstream as a considerable wave. As Fundy has the highest tides in the world the transformation of this normally placid stream can be quite dramatic. The Tourist Bureau will give you the daily arrival time.

Another unusual sight is at Hopewell Cape near the mouth of the Petitcodiac river. The force of the tides have carved mushroom-like columns from the soft limestone, rounded and narrow at the base, the tops are larger, like mushroom caps and have trees growing out of them. These are islands when the tide is in but when it goes out they look like giant flower pots—in fact that is what the local people call them.

Another local phenomenon is Magnetic Hill on the edge of town, a most curious place. You have to have a car to enjoy the strange experience. You start on Magnetic Hill Road at a white-painted post at the foot of the hill. You shut off your engine, put the car in neutral and it seems to coast up hill, gathering momentum as it goes. We tried this several times but it would not work for us—maybe because it was a wet, misty day. If you are lucky it is an odd experience and to add to your fun you can watch others trying to get the same effect. This tourist attraction is so well known that there is now a Magnetic Hill Inn where you can have a cup of coffee or meal while you watch people experimenting from a window.

Moncton was first settled early in the eighteenth century by German immigrants. Later Robert Monckton, who had recovered from being seriously wounded while serving under Wolfe in the battle for the Plains of Abraham, commanded a British Expeditionary Force which captured nearby Beausejour on the border with Nova Scotia, the first action in the Seven Years' War. The town was named after him but a clerical error in the corporation papers omitted the letter K.

During the summer the local Centennial Park offers scenic walks over woodland trails, tennis, swimming, picnics, pony rides and playground areas for children. In winter, you can enjoy sleigh rides, cross-country skiing, family skating, snowshoeing and tobogganing. The park's main entrance in St George Street is indicated by an old Pacific 5200 class CN steam locomotive. Moncton is the province's main railway centre and is known as the 'Hub of the Maritimes'.

Among the hotels in Moncton the best known is the Beausejour in Main Street. Out near Magnetic Hill, off the Trans-Canada Highway, there is a Wandlyn Motor Inn. This is one of a chain in New Brunswick and other provinces, a superior type of motel with good dining rooms, bar and swimming pool. The Keddy Motor Inns are another chain in Nova Scotia and New Brunswick. Recognizing that tourists are inclined to put on weight during their holidays, the latter feature an alternative low-calorie menu stressing nutritious food. Their chefs underwent a special course of instruction at Mount Saint Vincent University in Halifax, Nova Scotia, and, working with dieticians there evolved a series of special menus. A filet mignon, for example, with baked potato and vegetable of the day will have 455 calories.

The Fundy National Park faces the sea along a line of steep cliffs with irregular contours due to streams and waterfalls entering the bay. Inland the ground rises in a rolling plateau with forests, valleys and small lakes. There are more than 50 miles (80 kilometres) of hiking trails, motor boats are permitted in the bay and there are tennis courts, riding stable and golf course. Snowshoeing and cross country skiing are popular in the winter. Then there are the Fundy Islands, perhaps the best known being Campobello. Franklin Delano Roosevelt spent his summers there from 1905 to 1921 and his thirty-four room 'cottage' is now a museum.

One of the most interesting seaside resorts in New Brunswick is St Andrews. At the time of the American Revolution many Loyalists settled on the north shore of the Penobscot river believing that it would become the boundary and they were joined by others from along the coast as far as Boston. To their dismay the Penobscot was not selected but a river further north so they had to move again. This time they chose a peninsula in Passamaquoddy Bay which was to become St Andrews.

Unlike so many other Loyalists they had time to move many of their household goods and they hired sailing ships. An old bill shows an amount of £61 for 'dismantling and transporting a Coffee House'. In 1783 British Army engineers laid out the town and the people moved in with their baggage and furniture. More houses were built and the streets lined with chestnut and elm trees which are still there today. By the turn of the century, St Andrews had become fashionable as a summer resort with the arrival of the CPR. Sir William Van Horne built a summer residence and the CPR put up the Algonquin Hotel which now has its own golf course.

St Andrews has a most unusual church often said to have been 'the church that was born of an insult'. For the first thirty years all denominations were content to worship in the Anglican (Episcopal) church thanks to a broad-minded and beloved minister, the Reverend Samuel Andrews. After Mr Andrews' death in 1818 the Reverend John Cassilis, a clergyman from Scotland, became the first Presbyterian minister in St Andrews. He started to build a Presbyterian church and raised funds to do so from his congregation. Unfortunately there was only enough money to start the project. A cutting remark about Presbyterians' inability to go further, caused a Captain Christopher Scott to say that he would proceed with the work 'at his sole and individual cost' and by 1824 the Reverend John Cassilis led the first service.

The most striking thing in the church is the pulpit. It rises as high as the gallery and is made of bird's-eye maple and mahogany. The design was copied from a pulpit of a church in Greenock, Scotland, Captain Scott's home town. A gallery occupies two sides and the south west end, supported by pillars of bird's-eye maple. A large Scottish thistle is painted in each of the four corners of the ceiling. Outside, the building is in colonial style with a clock in the steeple and below it the carving of a spreading green tree. It is called Greenock Church—'Greenock' being a derivation of 'Green Oak'.

If you happen to be an amateur mineralogist or lapidarist you are probably aware that the Bay of Fundy region has long been a collecting area. At St Andrews along the shore line at low tide you can sometimes find nuggets of red and black granite, red and brown jasper, white and red-veined quartz, peridotite, agate, yellow, brown, grey and black flints. The appearance of the flint is unique to St Andrews because in the eighteenth and nineteenth centuries when ships were sailing for England with timber and fish, they returned with the hold full of flint from Dover as ballast. It was dumped along the shores; as years went by it was crushed and washed ashore and can now be picked up as smooth round pebbles. When polished they take on a lustre in multiple shades suitable for jewellery.

Prince Edward Island can be reached by either of two ferries. The one from New Brunswick runs from Cape Tormertine to Borden taking three quarters of an hour, and that from Nova Scotia goes from Caribou to Wood Island in one and a half hours. There are several direct flights from Montreal and Halifax daily. If you do fly in, many tourists drive around the province as Charlottetown airport has the usual rental agencies such as Tilden, Avis and Hertz. There is a choice of three excellent marked scenic routes to take according to the time you have and what you wish to see. The Blue Heron drive, which is the shortest, circles the island's centre segment signed with a white square with blue border and a blue heron in the centre. It takes in the farmhouse which was the setting for the book *Anne of Green Gables*. The Lady Slipper drive takes you through Summerside, second in size to Charlottetown, many little villages and the home of the Acadian descendents. The symbol to follow is a white square with red border and a red orchid in the centre. The third route is known as The King's Byway and its sign is a white square with a purple border and a crown in the middle. This will take you to the tip of the island and round to North Lake which is a major port for deep-sea fishing. Giant tuna can be up to 1,200 pounds (545 kilos) in weight and take hours to play. The landed fish becomes the property of the skipper but you can have photographs taken with your catch.

Prince Edward Island has many nicknames such as 'the farm sandwiched between two beaches', 'the million acre potato patch' and 'Canada's biggest camping ground', but many people just refer to it as PEI. Mostly it is the rolling farmland that people imagine but it is a surprise to find the rich soil is a deep red colour and the grass as green as in Ireland. The island is 140 miles (225 kilometres) long and 4 to 40 miles (6 to 65 kilometres) wide. You are never more than about a quarter of an hour's drive from a beach.

On the south shore lies Charlottetown, not a large place but with an historic background, for it was here in the Confederation Chamber of Province House, now a museum, that the Fathers of the Confederation held their first meeting in 1864. It is often said that the Prince Edward Islanders are like the insular British who, when the Channel is foggy, say that the Continent is cut off from Britain! Lord Dufferin meant somewhat the same thing with his quote that, when the island became a part of the Dominion in 1873, it was under the impression that it was annexing the rest of Canada! As the island was named after Queen Victoria's father and the capital after George III's queen there is no doubt about its Loyalist heritage.

In 1964 a modern Confederation Centre of the Arts was opened as a national memorial to the Fathers of Confederation. It has an art gallery, a library, a theatre to seat 1,000 people as well as a children's theatre and various art workshops. It is a pleasure for the visitor, who probably needs a rest anyway, to gain the feeling that life runs by quietly here. The older buildings remind one of Victoria. There is no madly rushing traffic, no jangling telephones and nobody appears to have frayed nerves. It is a pleasure for a change to dawdle over shopping, not to have to rush meals and to believe that perhaps the rat race is a myth. Family feuds do not seem to exist and it has been said that, although the legislature is made up of two parties, the only way to tell them apart is that one party is in and the other out. Perhaps they are like the Swiss in that nobody ever seems to know the name of the Swiss president. The cabinet nominates a different member each year, and a tale is told of a tourist who asked a passing Swiss in Basle the name of the president. The Swiss thought for a few moments and then his face broke into a smile. 'Actually I am this year', he said.

Seafood is delicious and if you like lobster you should enjoy yourself for they are mouthwatering and lobster suppers can be had practically anywhere during the season. They are even a tradition in church. At St Ann's church in Hope River the basement is licensed and the priest supervises the service! Before I stop praising the food I must, of course, mention the famous PEI potatoes which are succulent when roasted in their jackets. I had one perfectly shaped specimen at a restaurant and it had a tag inserted on a cocktail stick which read, 'I have been rubbed, tubbed and scrubbed, you can eat my skin.' The potatoes are really treated with respect. As a child I remember my father used to receive a case of them from a masonic friend of his in PEI. They arrived in a small orange box and, in the same way as with fruit, each potato was wrapped in crinkly tissue paper and was unmarked: no wonder they call them Prince Edwards.

PEI has popular appeal for the camper and caravanner because of its uncluttered shores and well organized facilities. They really understand tourism which, after agriculture, is their greatest source of revenue. The fishing villages and hamlets are charming and the welcome is warm. There is a well-run 'Dial-the-Island' reservation service which ensures that you get a place to stay. Thousands of visitors come to the island each summer. Even Jacques Cartier, after his many explorations, was enraptured by it and is quoted as saying—'It only needs the nightingale.'

8 NOVA SCOTIA — GATEWAY TO THE MARITIMES

East and west of Halifax there is water, for it is on a triangular tongue of land exactly in the middle of the Nova Scotia peninsula. On one side is the river-like North West Arm, on the other its famous harbour 6 miles (10 kilometres) long and 1 mile (1½ kilometres) broad. The capital of the province of Nova Scotia is still as Charles Dickens described it on arrival over a century ago.

I was dressing about half past nine next day, when the noise above hurried me on deck. When I had left it overnight it was dark, foggy and damp and there were bleak hills all around us. Now we are gliding down a smooth, broad stream at the rate of 11 miles an hour; our colours flying gaily; our crew rigged out in their smartest clothes; our officers in uniform again; the sun shining as on a brilliant April day in England; the land stretched out on either side, streaked with light patches of snow; white wooden houses; people at their doors; telegraphs working; flags hoisted; wharves appearing; ships; quays crowded with people; distant noises; shouts; men and boys running down steep places towards the pier; all more bright and gay and fresh to our unused eyes than words can paint them. We came to a wharf, paved with uplifted faces, got alongside and were made fast after some shouting and straining of cables, darted a score of us along the gangway almost as soon as it was thrust out to meet us and before it reached the ship and leaped upon the firm, glad earth.... The town is built on the side of a hill, the highest point being commanded by a strong fortress, not yet quite finished.

The fortress is complete today but has gone through many traumas since then. Happily a shot has never been fired in anger from the Citadel but it was shaken to its very foundations by the great Halifax explosion on 6 December 1917, when a munitions' ship collided with another in the harbour. Fire devastated most of the port and city and there were over 2,000 fatalities. The shock-waves were felt nearly 100 miles (160 kilometres) away. You can

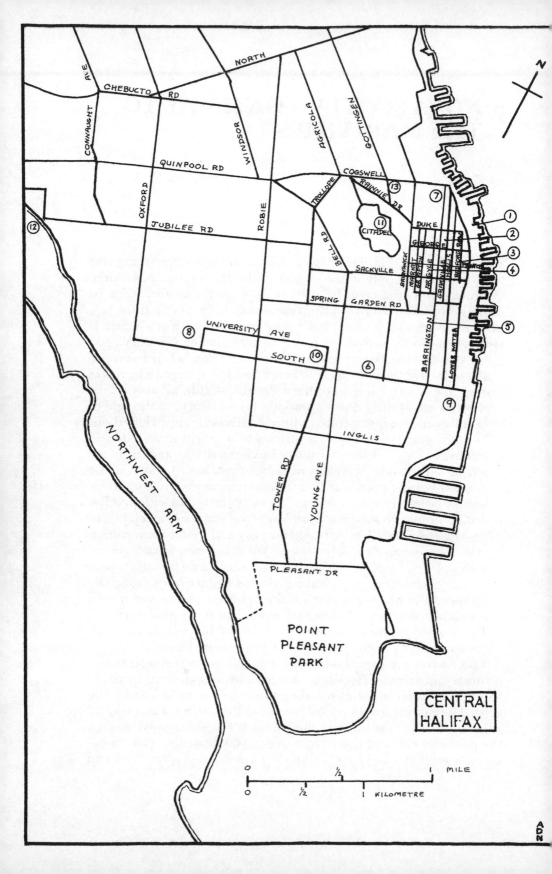

see newspapers and photographs of the holocaust in the Citadel, part of which is now an historical museum.

The Citadel is star shaped, like the one in Quebec, and with a similar sweeping view, for from it you can see over the city as well as the harbour with its two suspension bridges joining it to the city of Dartmouth. There is a toll of 25 cents either way. The Citadel has acted in many guises: as a jail (Leon Trotsky the Russian revolutionary, was held prisoner in 1917. One wonders what he thought of the harbour ammunition explosion), and it was a wartime detention centre, during the First World War. During the Second World War it was surrounded by anti-aircraft guns and searchlights and served as a signal post and radio station. In 1951 the fort was transferred to the then federal Department of Resources and Development, and five years later was created a National Historic Park. It is now administered by Parks Canada, Department of Indian and Northern Affairs and has a Centennial Art Gallery in the grounds. The firing of a noon-day gun is an old custom still carried on at the Citadel and in many other National Historic Parks in Canada.

Nearby is the Old Town Clock Tower, a replica of the original one built in 1803. The tower is in three tiers like a wedding cake. The bottom one is on pillars, the second one holds the clock and the top dome is the belfry. Because of the small space inside and the delicate nature of the mechanism the building is not open to visitors. Prince Edward, Duke of Kent, when he was Commander in Chief of the British forces, was rigid about punctuality and ordered the clock from London to keep the garrison soldiers and townspeople in mind of time. Perhaps the clock has the same effect

HALIFAX

Key to map

1	Historic Properties	8	Dalhousie University
2	City Hall. Grand Parade.	9	CN Station
3	Province House. Legislature.	10	Victoria General Hospital
4	St Paul's Anglican Church	11	Neptune Theatre
5	Government House. Lieutenant Governor's Residence	12	St Mary's family recreation centre
6	Chapel built in a day	13	Police Station
7	Chateau Halifax and Scotia Square		

today. You can certainly see it from many points in Halifax so there is no excuse for being late for an appointment.

Prince Edward also had a mansion with a separate music room built between Halifax and Bedford where he lived with Mme de St Laurent. The music room was a rotunda, thought to have been designed by William Hughes, Master Builder during that time at Halifax Dockyard. Built on a hillock it was a single room surrounded by a verandah supported by pillars. The mansion has gone but the music room remains. It is believed that a party was given in 1860 by the Prince of Wales, later Edward VII, when he visited the city, for the relatives of those who had been friendly to his father and Mme de St Laurent.

The slang term 'Bluenose' applied to the Nova Scotians originally comes from 'True Blue' and an intended insult by an American who said, 'Now the Loyalists have gone to live in such a cold place as Nova Scotia, they carry their colour in the middle of their faces.' Down through the years it seems to have become an affectionate term, especially after the wonderful career of the famous schooner of that name.

The 'Bluenose' was built in Lunenburg in 1921 to enter for the international Fisherman's Trophy race, won the previous year by the American schooner 'Esperanto'. At her first attempt she brought the cup back to Canada and she never lost it again in her twenty-year racing career. One after another she defeated the American schooners 'Elsie', 'Henry Ford', 'Columbia', 'Gertrude L. Thebaud', as well as a number of Canadian vessels built in an effort to surpass her remarkable abilities. All failed, in spite of the fact that the 'Bluenose', bearing the weight of increasing years, faced competition from sprightly young schooners. When she defeated the 'Thebaud' in her final races she sailed and handled as fast and as smartly as ever.

Under the hand of her famous skipper, Captain Angus Walters of Lunenburg, the 'Bluenose' won a permanent place in the hearts of the Canadians and carved a unique niche for herself in Canada's maritime lore. In spite of valiant efforts by her Captain and others to keep her in Canada, the schooner was sold as a freighter sailing in the West Indies. She foundered on a Haitian reef in 1946 however, but was not forgotten and on 23 July 1963, 'Bluenose II' was launched, her exact replica built in the same yard in Lunenburg and by many of the same men. Since the day she sailed from Lunenburg on 12 January 1964, 'Bluenose II' has proved a worthy successor to her namesake. Two days out of Nova Scotia on her maiden voyage to the West Indies, she fought for her life in winds of 80 to 100 mph (130-160 kph), gusting to 120 mph (190 kph). Captain Angus Walters, on board for the inaugural run, compared the storm to the worst he had ever experienced. She weathered the storm and many others since then. Today she cruises in Nova Scotia waters on sightseeing tours and private charters. When you are in Halifax there are of course regular cruise launches, but if you are lucky she will be waiting at the wharf adjoining Historic Properties which is her permanent berth.

Historic Properties, on the Halifax waterfront, is a fascinating spot for sightseeing, shopping and having a meal. During the 1960s the whole area, part of one of the longest waterfronts in North America, was about to be demolished to make way for a super highway. Fortunately a campaign to save it by local citizens was successful and many buildings have been restored to their original outside appearance while re-designing the interiors on two levels has resulted in the creation of more than forty retail stores, restaurants, pubs and offices.

If this sounds like a modern shopping mall I hasten to tell you it is not. The overall plan requires that the layout must conform as closely as possible to that of the original eighteenth and nineteenth centuries. The result is a surprising conglomeration of flights of steps, small rooms, oddly placed windows, beamed ceilings and haphazard exteriors connected by alleyways, arches and passages which is most pleasing to the eye.

The Halifax Gardens are beautifully landscaped with lily ponds and flower beds. Part of the park belonged at one time to the Horticultural Society so that, added to the native trees, there are others from China, Japan, Siberia, Europe and America. The bandstand was erected to celebrate Queen Victoria's golden jubilee, and ten years later for her diamond jubilee a fountain was unveiled. Another fountain was added in 1903 in honour of Nova Scotian soldiers who were killed in the South African War.

Point Pleasant Park is to the south of the city and is reserved by the Federal Government but is leased to the city for the traditional shilling a year for 999 years. There are several old forts and a martello tower and there is a bathing beach on the harbour side. 'Chain Rock' is so called because in the olden days to prevent enemy ships sailing up the North West Arm, a boom was laid across it with one end secured to ring bolts in the rock.

Of the city churches the oldest, an Anglican one, is St Paul's in Barrington Street built in 1750. St Matthew's in the same street is also very old and one of its ministers was a great grandfather of Grover Cleveland, a president of the United States. St George's Round Church is a rare example of circular ecclesiastical architecture reminiscent of those in Denmark. The church I found absorbing and quite unique was on South Park Street called 'Church That was Built in a Day', an appropriate name for that is just what happened. It was built of wood within 24 hours by the parishioners of St Mary's on 31 August 1843.

Province House in Hollis Street has an excellent library and valuable oil paintings. It is an impressive building which Charles Dickens is said to have called 'a gem of Georgian architecture'. I like the remark attributed to a retired Naval Officer who became Lieutenant Governor of Nova Scotia. He had been somewhat less than effusive in welcoming an official visitor who had taken the trouble to don full-dress uniform for the occasion and was not too pleased. 'I am sorry the fellow was offended,' the Governor said afterwards, 'but nobody interests me who arrives in Nova Scotia *by land.*'

The traditions of CP hotels are well maintained in the Chateau Halifax. You can lunch on top of the hotel in the Noon Watch restaurant, which at night for dinner becomes the Night Watch restaurant. The windows are angled downwards as in an airfield control tower to enhance the panorama of movement in the harbour below.

The top floor lounge is called Edward and Julie a suitably romantic choice when you remember the twenty-seven year liaison between Prince Edward and Julie de St Laurent which has already been mentioned with the music room.

In a corner of the dining room there is a bronze statue of Wolfe, said to have been on the staircase of the Chateau Frontenac. The bill of fare for the last dinner he gave before attacking Louisbourg in 1758 is in a glass case. At the top of the menu I noted:

47 plates   £17. 10. 0
20 bottles of Madeira at 5 shillings each — £5

I did not manage to write down the prices of the other courses but the total at the bottom read £98. 12. 6. More like the price of a good night out for four or six today!

The bar near the foyer is called Sam Slick's. He was one of the most popular characters in nineteenth-century literature and was the creation of Nova Scotian humourist, Thomas Chandler Haliburton. Long dead he is still Canada's foremost satirist and the vigour and variety of the opinions and experiences he expressed through Sam Slick, a clock maker, are as much fun today as they ever were. The English language is indebted to Sam Slick for some well-known sayings such as:

Six of one and half a dozen of another

As large as life and twice as natural

A nod is as good as a wink to a blind horse

Nothing is so heavy to carry as gratitude

If a man seems bent on cheating himself I like to be neighbourly and help him do it.

When ladies wear the breeches their petticoats ought to be long enough to hide them.

To display the variety of fare available in the Maritimes the Chateau Halifax sometimes organizes food festivals. Items on the menu include Acadian pan-fried fillet of sole, snow crab salad, a selection of scallop and lobster dishes and several special appetizers featuring Cape Breton oysters. Some of the desserts are crêpes stuffed with blueberries, Lunenburg apple tarts and Acadian gingerbread.

The recently built two-level Scotia Square with its boutiques, restaurants, uncluttered shopping centre and parking facilities, can be reached by escalators from the hotel foyer.

Dartmouth's written history dates back to 1749 and the founding of Halifax, but like many settlements on the shore of a great international harbour, it is inclined to be overshadowed by its sister city.

Dartmouth was the terminus of a great undertaking known as the Shubenacadie Canal, intended to connect Halifax Harbour with the Bay of Fundy through a 55 mile (88 kilometre) course of lakes and locks. It was started in 1826 but the work was abandoned ten years later after frosts had destroyed the stonework and money ran out. When a new company was organized in 1860, the Canal was opened at a small profit until about 1870. Today supertankers and container ships unload their cargoes and the gypsum carriers ply their never-ending trade from here to the ports of the world, but it is still Halifax that is referred to by mariners and business interests.

Peggy's Cove, about 30 miles (48 kilometres) from Halifax has been preserved as a typically charming fishing village — and it is.

It has a snug harbour but it really needs that lighthouse when mountainous waves wash over fishing boats seeking shelter. Artists love it and its pastel-shaded houses draw tourists like a magnet. It reminded me of Polperro in Cornwall or Sidi bou Said in Tunisia.

Strangely enough, not far from the diminutive fishing village of Peggy's Cove in St Margaret's Bay, tuna fishing is becoming big business. Most of us eat the small tuna fish which when caught weighs about 35 pounds (16 kilos), but the Japanese prefer 'fattened up' tuna, and their taste is now catered for here. The tuna fish likes a diet of mackerel and squid and fishermen tempt them with their favourite food so that they unknowingly swim into large nets. The nets are then drawn tight enclosing the tuna so that they can be directed into sea water 'corrals' where they can be intensively fed until they weigh between 50 and 100 pounds (23-45 kilos). The process takes some weeks and keeps the local fishermen busy catching the fish on which they feed. Tourists can visit the farm and see the tuna at close quarters.

When the fish have reached the desired weight it is essential that they are not damaged in any way and Japanese tuna experts are, so to speak, in at the kill. They shoot the tuna straight between the eyes. The dead fish must then be gently towed through the water to the shore, not in the usual way that deep-sea fishermen haul them out of the water and suspend them by the tail. Once the tuna reaches the beach it is carefully lowered into a coffin-like receptacle filled with ice to preserve it on its journey. It is dispatched by truck and plane to Tokyo reaching there within 48 hours. Immediately after arrival it is thinly sliced and put straight on the market where it fetches up to 45 dollars a pound. It is eaten raw—a rare delicacy indeed.

Lunenburg, west of Halifax, is built on a peninsula in Mahone Bay, next to St Margaret's Bay. This little shipbuilding and fishing town (population about 3,000) is famous not as much for 'Bluenose I' and 'Bluenose II' or her sea-faring past but because of untold treasure which has never been found. Nearby Oak Island, where it is supposed to be, would be a place where Long John Silver and his parrot would feel at home, for Treasure Island must have been like this. Covered with trees, the reason for its name and criss-crossed with sandy paths, the wooden shafts of underground workings stick up here and there and the island's only small bay is called Smuggler's Cove. It is joined to the mainland by a causeway so it is not strictly an island, but it has a decided air of mystery about it.

Men have dug and searched for gold and gems here for well over a century. It has always interested me how well-known treasures can completely disappear. What became of the Inca gold? What did Louis XVI and Marie Antoinette do with their crown jewels when they fled? Where are some of the world's best known portraits which have disappeared? It seems probable that if treasure is discovered on Oak Island, it may be that of Captain Kidd. This famous pirate offered to lead a ship to the place where he had hidden the treasure, accumulated during his East Indian days of privateering, in exchange for his life. The offer was made eleven days before he was to be hanged. He felt certain such a bargain would gain him pardon but the crown thought otherwise. Kidd was hanged, it is said, in an iron cage over Wapping Pier, the whereabouts of his treasure died with him and it has never been found — that is unless of course it is discovered on Oak Island.

In 1796 three men who were hunting on the island saw an old ship's block hanging from the branch of a sturdy oak tree evidently having been used as a derrick. Beneath it was a great depression about 30 feet (9 metres) in circumference. They fetched shovels from the mainland and began to dig and men have been digging ever since. They have uncovered layer after layer of oak wood planking, some overlaid with charcoal, down to a depth of 90 feet (27 metres), but flooding has always hampered the work. During the many borings a large variety of things have come to light: three oak chests — empty, fragments of vellum, chambers, tunnels, pits, some air locked but always in the end water has defeated the mining.

In 1909 Franklin D. Roosevelt was intrigued enough to back a company to investigate for two months. Expeditions of various kinds sank dozens more shafts in 1922, 1931, 1934, 1938, 1955 and in the sixties. In 1971 the first closed-circuit TV camera was lowered into what has come to be called the 'money pit'. Several people have died through accidents but still it is believed that treasure is there. The latest company, Triton Alliance Limited, is a mixture of Canadians and Americans who have been there during the seventies. How fantastic it would be if a treasure chest was finally discovered. When we visited the island it seemed quiet and ordinary but there is now a little museum with the oddments that have been discovered, maps, documents and photographs. You cannot drive on the little island but there is a large car park near the museum.

We stayed at the Oak Island Inn and were amused to hear that not only treasure is hidden on the island but there are also some interesting ghosts and the following notice appears in the dining room:

> Scientists believe that Ghosts haunt Oak Island without doubt; 7 ghosts are known. Some are apparent sights, some apparent sounds, some both. Each is thought to be a form of 'Time Independent Extra Sensory Perception' therefore, DO NOT USE cameras or tape recorders. Remember, describe forward observations, as they are often almost precisely like others before you. Scientific research is on going. One Ghost has been reported independently over 100 times. Be natural, be relaxed, be perceptive. The Ghosts that guard the millions are real.
>
> Peter Beamish, Ph.D.
> Bedford Institute
> Dartmouth, N.S.

Lunenburg's 1967 Centennial Project was a floating museum and visitors enjoy going aboard in the summer. She is the schooner 'Theresa E. Connor' which fished the Grand Banks for a quarter of a century bringing back tons of cod, cleaned, washed and salted. In 1963 her skipper was unsuccessful in getting enough men to fish from the dories and she was laid up. It should be explained that the method of fishing which was used was for a schooner to act as mother ship to a number or rowing boats, called 'dories'. These caught the fish by line and brought it back to the schooner for processing and storage. It was a hard and dangerous life far removed from the modern fleet of trawlers and factory ships which several countries use today to deplete the fishing grounds.

Instead of fish, the schooner's cargo is made up of trophies won by famous ships like 'Bluenose', nagivation instruments and neatly arranged fishing gear. Photographs depict life of the Lunenburg fishermen. The cabins are ship-shape with bunks made up, the galley table is laid and, still pinned to the bulkhead is a picture of King George VI and Queen Elizabeth. When you leave the ship there are still two more to see, one a Lunenburg member of the 'dragger fleet' and 'Reo II', an old-time rum runner. In the local Fishermen's Memorial Chapel there are long lists of names of men and ships who have been lost at sea during dreadful storms and the war years.

Annapolis Royal passed into the hands of the British in 1713 and became capital of the colony until Halifax was founded in 1749. Yet it was Samuel de Champlain who first set foot ashore there in 1604. Although none of the Champlain's original habitation remains, a re-creation has been built some 7 miles (11 kilometres) from the city. It has been painstakingly carried out and is considered a national historic site. It is open during the summer months and admission is free. This fur-trading post was the first European permanent settlement in North America, two years before Jamestown, Virginia, three years before Quebec and fifteen years before the Pilgrims at Plymouth Rock. The French called it Acadia.

The old British officers' quarters are now a museum open to visitors, and contain the Port Royal room, a Queen Anne room, a garrison room and a Haliburton hallway. The Acadian room was transferred bodily from an old homestead with wall boards and ceiling beams intact. It contains every utensil used in Acadian kitchens and their articles of clothing. The garrison room has many of the weapons and uniforms in common use more than a century ago.

The Annapolis Valley is one of the most celebrated apple-growing districts in the world. Long before Tasmania, south Australia and California began to grow apples it was known as the orchard of the Empire. The valley is sheltered on both sides by the North and South Mountains. Sunshine and soil combine to produce fruit, particularly apples, to perfection. The valley is a picture in the springtime when the blossoms are fully out and can be seen for miles clouding the soft landscape, but some people prefer it when the apple trees, laden down with fruit, are seen silhouetted against the blue water and sky. You get large and excellent fish in the many streams and lakes and during the spawning season it is fascinating to watch how the fish are caught in the Gasperau River. A long pole pivoted on a pylon at the river's edge has a counter-weight on the in-shore end and a net suspended from its four corners hangs from the end over a weir. The fisherman stands on a platform on the pylon so that he can see down into the water and the net is lowered into the weir to lie flat on the bottom. When a shoal is seen passing over the net a trip mechanism is released, the counterweight takes over and the net is whipped into the air full of fish. It is then swung over the bank and the fish are emptied straight into barrels. Some form of licensing is evidently used as the fishing has not depleted over the years.

The treaty after the Seven Years' War in Europe resulted in

Canada passing to the British. A harsh law was enacted which resulted in the forcible deportation of the French-speaking Acadians who, although they had been effectively under British rule since 1719, still kept their allegiance to France. It is a blot on the British conscience which has its present-day counterparts, and makes one wonder about the visiting of the sins of the fathers. Fortunately many with nowhere to go found their way back and a blind eye was turned to this, but the first exodus was a horrifying affair and nothing describes the tragedy more clearly than Longfellow's poem 'Evangeline' which is commemorated in an outstanding memorial at Grand Pré. It is in a most beautiful park and there is a little church and a charming statue of Evangeline, cast in bronze in Paris by a descendent of one of the first Acadian families to settle at Port Royal, Philippe Hebert. The sculptor executed it in 1918 but died before the work was finished. His son Henri completed the work and the statue was unveiled in 1920 by Lady Burnham. Looking at one side of the figure you see the young Evangeline. Walking around to the other you gradually see a saddened, much older Evangeline.

The park also has a bust of Henry Wadsworth Longfellow who created the legend of Evangeline during the period 1845-7. (It is strange to realize that he never set foot in Nova Scotia.) Evangeline brings to life the sorrow and tragedy of the removal of the Acadians through the loss of her lover who, like so many others, was deported before they could make any plans.

Evangeline's well is almost as engaging as her statue. Typical of those dug by the Acadians, it consists of a bucket counterpoised on a long pivoted pole exactly like the ancient Egyptian *shadoof* which visitors still see there today. The little Memorial Chapel with its pencil-thin steeple is believed to be over the site of an Acadian burial ground.

In Grand Pré village, high on a hill, there is the Church of the Covenanters, built by farmers during the eighteenth century. It has a high pulpit and old-fashioned box pews. There are a few other early buildings of British settlements still intact in the area. Near Horton Landing, a mile (1½ kilometres) east of Grand Pré, traces of dykes can be seen and an iron cross commemorating the deportation of the Acadians.

Not only the Loyalists swept across the border from America. Negroes came in large numbers from the American southern states in the ante-bellum slavery days. Nova Scotia was then the favourite asylum of coloured refugees. In 1904 there died in Hantsport,

William Hall, RM the first black VC and among the first of any race to win the Victoria Cross. He was born in Nova Scotia, the son of an escaped Virginian slave. At the Relief of Lucknow, during the Indian Mutiny, when the rest of the crew were killed by grape shot from the garrison, Hall continued single-handed to work his heavy naval gun until the wall was breached and stormed. A memorial to him in the form of a cairn with a plaque can be seen in the grounds of Hantsport Baptist Church. Hantsport is in the centre of an attractive farming area and is also the shipping port for gypsum, quarried near Windsor. There is a site called Observation Look-off on the banks of the Avon river from which you can watch the loading of the gypsum boats and the tides in the estuary.

If your interest lies in this direction you can obtain information from the Windsor Tourist Bureau. In this town, close to Hantsport, and on the same Avon estuary, there is an average tidal rise of 40 feet (12 metres) caused by the large flow in the Bay of Fundy, to which I have already referred, flooding in through the Minas Basin. In the days of old sailing ships you could expect to see a four master riding high against the quay and six hours later sitting on its keel on the mud flats. The Indians called the area 'Piziquid' — the 'Meeting of the Waters'. When the French settled here they built dykes and reclaimed the low lying marshland which is today very fertile.

Windsor is one of the most pleasant towns in the province, the seat of King's College and everlastingly associated with Judge Thomas Chandler Haliburton, the creator in the early 1800s of the mythical character Sam Slick who travelled around Nova Scotia selling clocks. As has already been mentioned he should never be forgotten as long as we use his maxims every day, such as 'Facts are stranger than fiction', 'It's raining cats and dogs', 'A miss is as good as a mile'. 'I wasn't born yesterday', and best of all 'You can't get blood out of a stone'. The Judge's charming house Clifton has been purchased by the Province as a museum.

The Windsor golf course has some interesting hazards such as the remains of old forts and moats, including the Fort Edward Blockhouse. The latter is in good repair despite the scars of golf balls. It served as a British base at one time and has a plaque to Flora MacDonald who helped Bonnie Prince Charlie to hide in several places before he escaped to Brittany. For this she was imprisoned in the Tower of London but eventually pardoned. She spent the winter of 1779 with her husband, Captain Alan MacDonald of the Royal Highland Emigrant Battalion, in

Windsor.

Cape Breton Island covers one seventh of Nova Scotia and is the province's most popular tourist area. It is joined to the mainland by the mile-long (1½ kilometre) Canso causeway. Ships from the Atlantic can pass through it into the Gulf of St Lawrence.

You can leave the Trans-Canada Highway at North Sydney and drive the 25-odd miles (40 kilometres) along Highway 22 to Louisbourg, a National Historic Park on the south-east coast of the island, probably the most interesting in the country and a highly successful tourist project, though it will take several more years to complete, for it involves the reconstruction of a whole fortified town which will become a piece of living history.

When the Treaty of Utrecht gave Britain the Atlantic coast of North America it did so with the exception of certain islands to be retained by the French. These included Prince Edward Island, St Pierre, Miquelon and Cape Breton Island; so Louisbourg was born, a township protected by walls connected by bastions named, King, Queen, Princess and Dauphin. Built to safeguard the Cabot Strait and St Lawrence waterway, it was attacked by New Englanders from the land side and fell. The attack was led by William Pepperrell as Commander in Chief. For his services he was created a baron in November 1746 — the only New Englander so honoured. He was active in raising troops during the 'French and Indian War' and received the rank of Lieutenant General in February 1759.

In 1748 the fortified town was returned to France but, only a decade later, Louisbourg was invaded again this time by General Amherst and his army, one of his officers being Brigadier James Wolfe. Louisbourg held out valiantly for five months but was eventually forced to surrender. The British were determined to erase the town completely. As in the way Carthage could not be totally destroyed by the Romans centuries earlier, neither could the British completely raze Louisbourg — foundations remained and today much of the old town is reborn and the rest will be in due course.

When King Louis XV originally built the town named after him he ruefully remarked that it cost him so much to build it that he expected at any moment to see its ramparts rise above the horizon at Versailles. It certainly is not costing much less to resuscitate today but *what* a worthwhile project. Eventually it will be comparable in stature to Williamsburg in USA. Buildings range from Governor's Palace down to taverns, and a fish market and a baker's shop with enticing aroma have been rebuilt. As soon as you arrive you are challenged by an officer and sentry costumed, as are all the people connected with the scheme, in eighteenth-century dress. Suddenly you are drawn back to a vanished way of life and involved in a most unusual experience.

From Louisbourg to Baddeck by road is about 70 miles (112 kilometres) as you have to return by Highway 22, bypass Sydney and take route 105, but it is well worthwhile not only because of the scenic drive but because, in the village of Baddeck, you can visit the fascinating museum of Dr Graham Bell. He can be likened to a modern Michelangelo as, although not a painter, he also tackled the problem of mechanical flight, invented an instrument for transmitting sound by variation in a beam of light, perfected Edison's phonograph and, his greatest triumph, invented the telephone. Shaw used the system of voice therapy which Bell had devised for his heroine in his play *Pygmalion* and indeed Bell made great strides forward with deaf aids helped by his beloved wife who was deaf from birth.

Graham Bell loved Cape Breton and built himself a nine-roomed house on Beinn Bheagh (beautiful mountain) where he carried out his work overlooking the water and aerial experiments with his 'Silver Dart' to which there is a memorial.

He experimented with kites and inspired the men who first tried to fly in 1909. His work included desalinating sea water to help those who might be shipwrecked. He also devised bullet detectors, iron lungs and a forerunner of the modern hydrofoil boat. His motto, carved on a wall in the museum, sums up his ambitions. 'The inventor is a man who looks around upon the world and is not contented with things as they are. He wants to improve whatever he sees, he wants to benefit the world; he is haunted by an idea.'

Much of the atmosphere of the Graham Bell museum is achieved by Victorian photographs. It was interesting to see one of Queen Victoria who had placed her foreshortened arm across the back of a chair so that the defect was unnoticeable.

The scenery in the north of the island is lovely, much of it being a national park. The 180 miles (about 280 kilometres) circular drive along the Cabot Trail is spectacular, especially in the autumn when the maple leaves vary in colour from purple to pink and yellow. This part of the island has been likened to the Scottish Highlands, save for the maple trees, but it could also be compared with Italy's Amalfi drive with its rugged, sheer coastline or the lacets of

Switzerland. Perhaps the best comment was made by a Canadian in three words—'Don't miss it!'

A cairn to the memory of John Cabot has been placed at Cape North, with a bust of him looking out to sea wearing a tricorn hat. There are well-kept picnic sites and hiking paths with wonderful views and you may be fortunate to see a caribou, bear or lynx. The Scottish traditions are very strong in Cape Breton and there are festivals with highland dancing and piping. Island crafts include hand-knitted sweaters, crocheted shawls, quilts, afghans, dolls, ceramics and pottery.

One evening we shall not forget was when we arrived at Keltic Lodge at Ingonish Beach at sunset. The hotel is owned by the government and is in a beautiful situation on a spit of land which forms part of a millionaire's estate. It is rated as the best seasonal hotel in the island and maintains a high standard of cuisine. It was a warm evening and we decided to go for a walk in a wood at the back of the hotel. We were wandering along a pathway when something made me look to one side and there sitting a few yards away was a most magnificent fox. He was reddish in colour, his ears pointed, amber eyes looking steadily at us. His front paws were tucked between his back legs and his brush lay still behind him. His fur gleamed in the sunshine. We stood still, fascinated. I said softly that I would try and take his picture but as I moved my hand to reach for my camera he got up and came towards us. We stood rooted to the pine needles and I just left my hand on the camera strap. He came closer and then walked off into the trees. The following morning when we were saying farewell to the manager I told him about our fox. He was not at all impressed. 'Oh,' he said casually, 'we all love animals here and we can't keep pets as we only open in the summer months. This spring someone shot a vixen near here and we were furious as she had cubs. Well, we just left food out for them and now they are as tame as dogs. You obviously met one of them.'

To me the most endearing Canadian animal is the beaver. I well remember the first time an uncle took me on a lake to see one of their houses. As we got closer a large beaver swam out towards us and then hit the surface of the water with a loud slap of his flat tail. It made a crack like a rifle shot which was to warn the beaver family that we were approaching. You can tame a beaver in the same way as an otter and they have similar endearing habits.

Beavers are very industrious animals and go to great lengths to improve their surroundings by damming streams. To do this they fell trees by standing on their hind legs and gnawing round the trunk which unfortunately leaves a sharp stump and this can be a menace to the unwary if in long grass. They drag the trees in their mouths to their dam site, collect mud and stones in their front paws for reinforcement and in this way control the depth of the pools where they build their houses. The entrance to these is always under water but a tunnel leads upwards to a dry house dug out above water level. To prevent the cubs from straying a shelf is made in the house in which they are placed when the parent beavers swim out to forage for food. When a beaver is on a bank and wishes to be dry he can wring his fur out on either side with his forepaws. One man we heard of trapped a couple of beavers for a zoo and put them in a wooden box. While he was fetching his car they bit their way through and scampered back to their lake!

9 NEWFOUNDLAND—ATLANTIC OUTPOST

St John's lies mainly in a giant saucer whose sides rise up round a landlocked harbour. If you do not fly in by Air Canada or Eastern Provincial, the best way to get an overall glimpse of the Newfoundland capital is from Signal Hill which rises high above the side of 'The Narrows', the harbour entrance. You will be on historic ground, nowadays a national park, for it was here that Marconi received his first transatlantic wireless signals from a sending station he had set up in Cornwall in 1901. In 1904 he entered into an agreement with the British Post Office for the commercial transmission of wireless messages and in the same year, through the same means, the first ocean daily newspaper was started on the ships of the Cunard line. In 1906 he invented a new persistent wave system of wireless telegraphy and established a service for public use between England and America. One of his sayings was that 'Nothing is impossible, you just have to find out the way to do it.'

Cabot Tower on its high bluff was built in 1900 for Queen Victoria's diamond jubilee and to celebrate the four hundredth anniversary of John Cabot's discovery of Newfoundland. When you could cross to Newfoundland from Europe by ship it was the first thing you saw as you approached 'The Narrows'. People who have never seen it in reality know it well as it has been reproduced many times on Newfoundland stamps. Made of red sandstone it is small, 30 feet (9 metres) square and 50 feet (15 metres) high and is built over the site of an old blockhouse. The eighteenth and nineteenth century fortifications on Signal Hill have long since gone and only a few ancient guns point their muzzles out over the Atlantic. One is used as the 'Noonday Gun' and is fired every day.

Although enemy U boats came close to the harbour mouth in the Second World War the only notorious visitors since have been fantastically beautiful—icebergs. Formerly a hazard to shipping, especially in foggy conditions, today they can be seen on radar screens and avoided. With their white and turquoise pinnacles they are spectacular watched from the land as they drift in the currents, occasionally losing their balance and doing a giant somersault. This is caused by the fact that most of the iceberg is below the surface where it gradually melts until the centre of gravity changes and it assumes a new attitude. I once saw this happen and it seemed to create a minor tidal wave. On another occasion, coming up from the Gulf of St Lawrence with my parents by ship on a foggy night, the note of the foghorn suddenly changed dramatically. 'That was the echo from an iceberg,' someone said quietly and we all held our breath until the next blast resumed its normal dismal tone.

On a sunny day the city of St John's, clustered around the inner rim of the harbour, is a maze of painted wooden houses with church steeples above them, those sheathed in copper a glimmering pale green. Higher still rise the twin towers of the Roman Catholic Cathedral and the Confederation building. In the distance there is a theatrical backdrop of hills. A favourite night drive is to take visitors up to Cabot Tower. The city looks lovely in the moonlight with its necklaces of street lights, flashing signs and illuminated windows twinkling in the water. Chain Rock at the harbour entrance has a tiny lighthouse. In the 1700s a chain could be bolted across from it to the other side in the same way as in Halifax.

Halfway down Signal Hill there is a building called the Interpretive Centre which has interesting audio-visual displays giving a mini history of the capital and describing the various skirmishes between the French and British. The last fighting between the two occurred here at the end of Europe's Seven Years' War. Before leaving Signal Hill I must relate one British-French confrontation which did not take place. It was in the year of 1796 and whether the story is fact or apocryphal I am not certain. The British used a deceptive ruse as follows.

The garrison in St John's, small and badly armed, received a signal that French battleships had been sighted in the Atlantic making their way towards St John's harbour. The commander thought quickly and ordered that all red flannel and other red material should be bought or commandeered. It was hurriedly cut into strips and sewn on the coat fronts of both men and women who then lined the heights of Signal Hill. As the French ships sailed towards 'The Narrows' and when the sailors scanned the hills they saw what they took to be battalions of red-coated British soldiers and hurriedly withdrew.

A similar stratagem was successfully used in Malta during the Great Seige by the garrison commander at Mdina and it would be interesting to know if he had conceived the idea himself or heard of the Newfoundland one or vice versa. In the case of the Maltese there happened to be a large store of uniforms which had never been issued and all the townfolk wore them, including the women. The Turks seeing an army awaiting them on the Mdina Heights also turned back.

St John's is one of the oldest of cities in North America and, despite having been ravaged by fire several times, somehow retains its own special atmosphere together with some of its early buildings and streets. The Colonial Building, Government House, the Roman Catholic Basilica of St John the Baptist, the splendid National War Memorial and the Anglican Cathedral, to name a few, have all been through many vicissitudes but have kept their own ambience even though the latter has been gutted by fire and renovated. It was designed by Sir Gilbert Scott whose genius is admired or deplored in London according to whether people approve or disapprove of such buildings as the Albert Memorial and St Pancras Station. Be that as it may the Anglican Cathedral is considered one of the finest in North American and has a small museum.

St Thomas's Church in Military Road, dating from the 1800s is a fine example of colonial architecture. It was at one time the garrison church of nearby Fort William which stood where the Newfoundland Hotel stands today. Patrick Kough was the architect. He came from Wexford in Ireland and was in Newfoundland as a 'supervising constructor' for Government House which is only a five-minute walk from the church. In 1846 a great gale moved St Thomas's which is built of wood, 6 inches (15 centimetres) on its foundations and, to stabilize it, wings were added on the north and south sides. In 1817 it became an ordinary civilian church. Traditionally the Governors of the island have a pew here, at one time in a small gallery with armchairs. There is still a military feeling about it and some frayed regimental flags hang from the vaulting.

The Commissariat just behind St Thomas's Church was both residence and working quarters for the Assistant Commissary General. In early days it was cheek by jowl with the commanding officer's private quarters and Fort William. In 1872 the Government leased it to St Thomas's Church as a rectory which it remained until 1969. It is now a charming museum furnished as it was in

1820. It is quite large with two storeys over a cellar. The ground floor has the usual offices and a kitchen, the second floor a drawing room, dining room and two bedrooms, the third floor has four bedrooms.

Government House, completed in 1831, is a rectangular building set in spacious grounds. It is two storeys high consisting of a centre block and two wings. It is surrounded by a shallow moat for no more warlike reason than that it was thought at one time this would discourage snakes. Fortunately there are none in the island and part of the moat is now utilized as a basement. The ceilings in the principal rooms were painted by a Polish prisoner, a fresco artist who had tried to pass fraudulent cheques. He was put to work painting the ceilings not only of Government House but also of the Colonial Building and the Court House. In return his sentence was remitted by one month!

The Colonial Building is close by Government House and on the same side of Military Road. It is just inside the entrance of Bannerman Park. Its façade is of cut limestone from Cork and it has a handsome Ionic portico. It served as home for the Newfoundland Government for 110 years and how houses the Newfoundland public archives.

Military Road, as the name implies, is one of the earliest in the city and it linked Fort William with the town's most important buildings. Eventually Fort Townshend was built and the garrison headquarters was moved there. This unlike Fort William, has the same thing said about it as many other Canadian forts: 'it never fired a shot in anger'. When the garrison was withdrawn in 1871 the fort became the Police Headquarters.

The Basilica of St John the Baptist was completed in 1855. In Romanesque style, it is built of Irish limestone and Newfoundland granite from Conception Bay. Its twin towers, one with a clock, are 138 feet (42 metres) high. On its one hundredth anniversary it was created a Minor Basilica. Inside it is very ornate, the mouldings and pendants being coated with gold leaf. Of the many statues and treasures it has, one is most interesting and oriental. Mohamed Ali, Khedive of Egypt, presented Pope Gregory XVI with some Egyptian marble which adorns parts of St Paul's in Rome. Two slabs that were left over were imported for the Basilica and now form part of the high altar.

Water Street is the oldest part of the city and has always been the main shopping area until recently when it has been superseded by suburban shopping malls. It literally borders the harbour front and there is always a salt tang in the air. The ornate War Memorial is not far from the Newfoundland Hotel and just above Water Street. A plaque on it records a sentence written by Rudyard Kipling: 'Close to this commanding and historic spot Sir Humphrey Gilbert landed on the 5th day of August 1583 and, in taking possession of the new found land in the name of his sovereign Queen Elizabeth, thereby founded Britain's overseas empire.' Along Water Street on the landward side you pass the Court House. It can be reached by flights of stone steps. The cornerstone was laid by the Duke and Duchess of Cornwall, later King George V and Queen Mary. Originally the building was used by the Prime Minister, the Colonial Secretary and the Cabinet.

There are no chateau-like or highrise hotels in St John's but it is a cosmopolitan city and offers pleasant accommodation up to international standard. The best place to stay is the Battery Inn on Signal Hill which has the usual cocktail lounge, coffee shop, sauna and pool. The dining room has splendid views especially attractive at night when you gaze out over the city. The Newfoundland Hotel is run by CN and is in Cavendish Square. Its dining room is called The Captain's Table.

An excellent place to eat in Water Street is the Starboard Quarter overlooking the harbour. The lobsters and fish are delectable. For a quick lunch or snack Bowrings Department Store on Water Street has a cafeteria which overlooks the harbour.

From Water Street it is about 10 miles (16 kilometres) to Cape Spear, which is the most easterly point in North America with Ireland 1,640 miles (2,640 kilometres) distant. At the foot of the lighthouse, believed to be the oldest in North America, there are some guns and bunkers left from the Second World War.

The Confederation Building, seat of Government since union with Canada, has a military museum at the top where you can see models of Forts William and Townshend, firearms, and military trappings. It recalls to mind Gertrude Stein's famous remark—'The things I most enjoy about museums is looking out of the windows.' This really is true at this museum because the Confederation Building is on higher ground at the edge of the city and thus commands a magnificent view over it. This includes the heights on either side of the narrow harbour entrance though you cannot see down into the saucer of the harbour itself. When last there I watched a bank of white fog creep in through 'The Narrows' over the harbour, yet inland the sun continued to shine. Because of the warm Gulf Stream meeting the cold Atlantic it not only brings icebergs round the island but banks of fog. This has always caused headaches to shipping although often, in the island itself, the weather can be sunny and clear.

I attended a school in England and shall always remember the stir I caused when I first arrived. I only found out the reason much later. Although there were girls from various parts of Europe, I was the first Newfoundlander so some of them decided they had better consult their dictionaries—let me hasten to add not the Oxford dictionary but the little ones which you get in Italian and French for learning English. One girl found 'Newfoundland—a type of dog', another 'Island cut off by fog' and the third 'Labrador is part of the island'. The girl who had the latter firmly believed I would turn out to be an Eskimo! The only remark that really hurt was when I was looked over with disgust and told, 'You are just ordinary!'

The rest of the Confederation Building is as interesting as the museum. An attendant will take you to the House of Assembly on the ninth floor. The Newfoundland coat of arms is over the Speaker's Chair and was granted by Charles I in 1637. It shows two Beothuck Indians holding a shield which bears a rampant lion and unicorn. The shield is surmounted by a moose and the motto is 'Seek ye first the kingdom of God.' Even more interesting than the furnishings is the fact that they are mostly gifts from other Canadian provinces to mark the occasion on 31 March 1949 when Newfoundland became Canada's tenth province. The mace is from British Columbia, other gifts include the Speaker's Chair, tables and a wall clock.

When you leave the Confederation Building there are two interesting statues to see, one of Sir Wilfred Grenfell and the other John Cabot. Sir Wilfred, born in Chester in 1868, was both a missionary and a medical doctor. He was brilliant but modest and came to Newfoundland after the great fire in St John's in 1892 to superintend the Royal National Mission to Deep Sea Fishermen. By 1913 he had formed his Grenfell Association, which raised money for the town he created and which he named after his patron saint—St Anthony. He had great personal charm and always managed to raise money for his schemes. He even persuaded Walt Disney to make a short cartoon with a seal as the hero. He found the most appalling poverty in northern Newfoundland and Labrador and nothing deterred him from 'making things right'. He founded a hospital, handicraft industry, farms, schools and orphanages. He introduced Lapland reindeer as meat and draft animals but they did not thrive. One man who knew him told me that he never hesitated to do something himself if there was no one else, even if he had little idea how to do it. Sir Wilfred died in 1940 but his name will never be forgotten and to this day Grenfell nurses, who come from all over the world, continue his hospital work. He was a great visionary, an early Schweitzer.

There are photographs and displays depicting Newfoundland's sea-going history in the Maritime Museum. This forms part of the recently built Arts and Culture Centre in the newer northern area of the city. Here also there are a 1,000-seat auditorium offering concerts and plays all year round, an art gallery and a library. The centre commemorates Canada's one hundredth birthday and its restaurant, called Act III, has a delightful ambience.

Memorial University in St John's, founded as a college in 1925, to the memory of the Newfoundlanders who died in the First World War, was granted full university status in 1949, and in 1961 it was officially opened by Eleanor Roosevelt. One of its outstanding Chancellors was Lord Thomson of Fleet.

On the eastern side of St John's there is a lake called Quidi Vidi (pronounced 'Kiddy Viddy') from which a stream runs into a small fishing village clustered round a sea inlet both of the same name. It has a little fort of its own and an historic wooden building that was used as a dressing station for the wounded during the fighting between the French and English. The harbour entrance is very narrow and steep-sided and during the Napoleonic wars a plan was made to dynamite the sides and fill it in for fear of it being used in an attack on St John's. The local fishermen were furious and the plan was dropped.

During the last war, after the signing of the Lend-Lease agreement, many Americans were stationed in Newfoundland and an air force base was constructed along the shore of Quidi Vidi lake, named Fort Pepperell after Sir William Pepperell, already mentioned, who led the attack on Louisbourg. When the lease expired it was returned to the city and renamed Pleasantville.

Since 1828 the great festival of the year in St John's has always been Regatta Day, on the first Wednesday in August—weather permitting. If not, it is postponed until the first suitable day which used to be announced by the additional firing of the noon-day gun.

It is always called 'The Day of the Races' on the 'pond'. The bank on the north side of the lake sloping to the water's edge is packed with people and various racing flags fly from a line of white tents. As a child I remember my grandfather, who was on the committee, wearing a black silk hat and frock coat, sitting with similarly attired gentlemen, driving around in a shiny carriage drawn by black satiny horses to the committee tent. As the first race left the starting point and the band struck up 'The Banks of Newfoundland', everyone shouted and cheered. There were always so many races that someone you knew was bound to win so the day ended happily for all.

Bowring Park is one of the prettiest small parks in Canada and you can drive around it. It was designed in 1911 by a Dutch landscape artist, Rudolph Cochius, who came to St John's to do the work, fell in love with Newfoundland and remained there. He chose various species of shrubs, trees and flowers which have blended in together over the years. You pass over a bridge to enter the park and the road takes you along the bank of a river. As you round a curve you see a bronze caribou standing on an outcrop of rock in the shade of some trees. He looks alive and friendly and was designed by Bail Gotta in memory of the many men of the Newfoundland Regiment who were killed in 1916 at Beaumont Hamel when only sixty-eight survived. A replica of the caribou stands at Beaumont Hamel. As you drive along you catch a glimpse of a low bungalow where kings and queens and other dignitaries have been entertained in the past. It is a delightful place to stop for afternoon tea. Through the trees a little further on there is the statue of a soldier called The Fighting Newfoundlander, also by Bail Gotta, which has been reproduced on Newfoundland stamps. Here and there you will notice trees with small plaques recording the person who planted them. One has the name of Viscount Alexander of Tunis, 29 April 1949 and it was planted during his inaugural visit as Governor General to Canada's tenth province.

Perhaps the most endearing statue of all is that of Peter Pan, just the way he stands in Kensington Gardens by the Serpentine. He is a copy of Sir George Frampton's original statue. I know of one other which stands in a small park near the Hilton Hotel in Brussels, a present from the children of London to the children of Brussels. The one in Bowring Park has an inscription on the base which reads: 'In memory of a little girl who loved the park.' The girl was Betty Munn, a godchild of Sir Edgar Bowring who sponsored the park. She was drowned in an accident at sea.

Having seen so many shopping malls in other cities it was interesting to be invited to the opening of the largest regional shopping centre in Atlantic Canada. Called The Village, it is on two storeys and has ninety-six shops. Huge skylights flood the concourses with daylight. The main 'thoroughfare' has a waterfall and mini park complete with benches. Tropical trees some reaching up to 25 feet (8 metres), shade strollers from sun or electric light.

The opening ceremony was in the evening. Bars had been set up in the arcades, a dance band played and a cold supper of lobster, salmon, cold meats and salads was served. The evening festivities ended with speeches and a huge iced cake being cut by Lewis Ayre, a banker and director of several Newfoundland firms. There was the inevitable 'fly in the ointment' next morning when several snakes were discovered in the earth surrounding the tropical trees shipped from Florida. They were soon rounded up but certainly lent an air of added excitement.

As Newfoundland is the nearest point of the North American continent to Europe it is not surprising that flying has played a great part in its history since pioneering days. Alcock and Brown made the first successful flight across the Atlantic in a converted Vickers Vimy bomber from Lester's Field in St John's to Clifden, Ireland. Fortunate in having tail winds they managed the flight in 16 hours and 12 minutes, a record that was not beaten for over a decade. Charles Lindbergh took his point of departure from Cabot Tower on his solo flight from New York to Paris in 1927, and in 1933 landed on Quidi Vidi Lake.

Early aircraft either took off from pasture land like Lester's field or from the water but finally an airstrip was built in the island at Harbour Grace and famous fliers like Kingsford Smith used it. My father, whose firm in the early days was the agent for Trans-Canada Airlines, often flew with Captain Douglas Fraser, one of Newfoundland's pioneer airmen. On one never-to-be-forgotten occasion he took me to Harbour Grace to meet Amelia Earhart before she took off on one of her flights.

Numerous people who have not visited Newfoundland know Gander, not usually because of its salmon fishing which is excellent, but because of its airport. The earlier scheduled transatlantic flights using aircraft of limited range used to stop there to refuel. Today its main purpose, apart from being a busy domestic airport and housing the western terminal of the transatlantic flight control system, is as an emergency field. It reached its heyday in the last war when American-built bombers were being ferried to the United Kingdom and at one time were leaving as frequently as one every two minutes. Gander lake was also used for a flying boat service which carried VIPs. Should you touch down at Gander today the airport museum is interesting but if you have time for a short walk from the airport buildings there is a wartime Lockheed Hudson bomber set up as a memorial close by and its plaque tells the story.

> ATLANTIC FERRY: Pilot Memorial. Air Vice Marshal D. C. T. Bennett C.B., C.B.E. and D.S.O. was the Captain of a Lockheed Hudson bomber which departed Gander 22.33 G.M.T. on the night of November 10th 1940 and landed at Aldergrove Ireland 09.45 G.M.T. the next morning. The aircraft here is identical to the one that made the flight which was the first successful Trans Atlantic crossing from Gander. It is mounted here on the site in commemoration of that event and the many thousands of men and aircraft who have followed since then — 'Better be not at all than not be noble.'

While on the subject of pioneering, Captain Bob Bartlett, the Arctic explorer, was born in the fishing village of Brigus. As a youngster he skippered one of his father's fishing boats to Labrador and from this beginning, became a leading navigator through the ice floes. He started sailing with Robert Peary in 1898 and captained one of his ships on various polar expeditions. In 1908 on leaving Sydney, Nova Scotia on the 'SS Roosevelt', he left the port for the North Pole, a unique clearance. The Roosevelt sailed to within some 500 miles (800 kilometres) of the pole and he then accompanied Peary across the ice by dog team until ordered back to his ship.

In 1917 Bob Bartlett helped rescue an expedition in Greenland and continued to make voyages into the Arctic well into the 1930s, receiving a long list of honours from various countries.

About an hour and a half's drive from St John's along the Trans-Canada Highway you reach Placentia, the old French capital of Newfoundland. In those days it acted as guardian of the sea route from Europe to the Great Lakes. It was at Argentia, a peninsula projecting into the bay just outside Placentia harbour, that Churchill and Roosevelt met aboard a warship in 1941 to issue the Atlantic Charter guaranteeing the Four Freedoms to all peoples of the earth once the Anglo-American victory over the Axis powers was complete.

In the centre of the west coast, Corner Brook is the island's second largest town, sometimes called the 'Western Capital'. It began as a planned town site for pulp and paper mill workers and has thrived through the years. It is in a most attractive setting which includes the famous Humber river teaming with salmon. The scenery in this part of the island is lush and spectacular. Northward past Deer Lake there is Bonne Bay and Gros Morne National Park, a wonderful place for holidays and fishing.

In the centre of the island are the twin towns of Windsor and Grand Falls which, like Corner Brook, sprang up originally round the paper pulp industry based on the vast spruce forests. The late Lord Northcliffe, owner of the Daily Mail, lived in a house here modelled on one built for his friend Mark Twain. A museum in Grand Falls is devoted to the history of the Beothuk Indians who were the first inhabitants. One of their last survivors, Shananditti, was captured by John Payton, given the English name of Mary March and shown every kindness, but she died after two years.

Newfoundland may not be the largest or have the biggest population of Canada's provinces but it has a charm for the visitor which is all its own. Even today it is comparatively unspoiled and if you are looking for a holiday which includes fishing, shooting, camping and getting away from it all it has much to offer.

There is one aspect of the province which I cannot omit. It is to Canada what Ireland is to the English, the source and subject of many and far-fetched tales. The fisherman is portrayed as a simple soul lacking in education, which he no longer is, but the legend persists and provides a fund of laughter and enjoyment. Here is an example.

An old lady, a fisherman's wife, reached her hundredth year and was asked if she would be interviewed on the radio. She was delighted. The young announcer was fascinated with stories of her life and the fact that she had never been ill. His final question was, 'You mean to say that in all your life you have never been bedridden?' 'Indeed I have,' was the quick retort, 'hundreds and hundreds of times, young man — and twice in a dory!'

10 FOOD AND DRINK

Half the pleasure for tourists visiting a country for the first time is tasting unusual food or eating dishes they already know but cooked in a different way. Instead of keeping their recipes secret, Canadians enjoy sharing the intricacies of their delicious cooking with newcomers. If you are invited out to breakfast, it may mean an early start to the day and may turn out to be what they call a 'working breakfast'. Businessmen with tight schedules tend to do this and skip lunch or just have a snack. Although we know a continental breakfast means coffee or tea with croissants, butter and jam, a working breakfast in Canada can mean eggs and bacon and perhaps a fish course, hot muffins and coffee or tea.

Eating and slimming simply do not marry unless you have great willpower to refuse Canadian desserts and cakes. At least with the following recipes you can have one dish at a time or try out some on different days and thereby not increase your calorie count.

I have written about the superb menus at La Sapinière in Val David in Quebec where Marcel Kretz is the chef. Here are a few of his favourite recipes.

The cup measurement used here is any suitable household cup.

VICHYSSOISE   *Serves 6*
This soup can be served hot or cold. It is actually a plain leek and potato soup.

2 medium leeks, minced	1 cup heavy cream
1 medium onion, chopped	1 cup milk
5 medium potatoes, sliced very fine	Salt, white pepper
4 cups chicken stock (or water)	Garnish: Chopped chives

Sauté leek and onions lightly, add potatoes, cover with water or chicken stock, add seasoning, let simmer for 20 minutes or until well cooked. Let cool and put through sieve or blender. Add cream and milk and chopped chives as garnish.

CLAMCHOWDER 'GASPESIENNE'   *Serves 4*

In the Gaspè Peninsula, potatoes are widely used in many fish preparations. It is almost the only vegetable to grow easily in this part of Quebec.

½ cup leek, minced   ½ cup potatoes, diced
½ cup celery, diced   3 cups clams (baby clams
1 small onion, chopped   if possible)
5 cups water or light fish stock 1 tbsp butter
                                  Salt, pepper, thyme, bayleaf

Sauté lightly in butter all the vegetables, except the potatoes, add 5 cups of water or light fish stock, use also the liquid from the clams if these are canned, add potatoes and seasoning. Simmer until all the ingredients are almost cooked. About 5 minutes before they are well cooked, add the clams. Fresh or frozen clams can also be used but, being sometimes quite hard, they should be minced or chopped accordingly. Do not overcook.

Marcel Kretz says, 'Fish to me has become a "way of eating". With new ways of transportation and refrigeration, fish in its best eating condition is now available everywhere and to every possible taste. In our hotel the consumption of fish and other sea products has increased by 50 per cent in the last three years and represents now nearly 40 per cent of our total meal sales. Information by all possible media and consumer groups has been partly responsible for this trend.'

PIKE MOUSSELINE   *Serves 4*

If it is difficult to get a small quantity of pike use sole, cod, halibut, pickerel or perch. This of course alters the taste of the final product, but still is a good substitution.

9½ oz (250 g) pike   6 eggs
5½ oz (150 g) cream 35 per cent   5½ oz (150 g) butter
   weight   Salt, white pepper, juice of
                                     1 lemon

Put fish fillet twice through the meat grinder. Mix the ground fish in a mixer, blender or mixette with softened butter and eggs, add seasoning and lemon juice. Beat for 10 minutes and put in refrigerator for 15 minutes. Take out, add cream and beat for another 10 minutes.

Butter four small casserole dishes and fill them up, half way only, with the mixture. Place them in a pan with water (bain marie), cover and let simmer *very slowly* till the mousseline gets firm. This should take 20-30 minutes.

This mousseline can be used just as it is, as stuffing for sole fillets (paupiettes) or for boned trout. It is delicious served with a sauce Newburg.

SAUCE NEWBURG
With the fish trimmings (skin, bones, head) make a fish bouillon. Don't forget to add the usual herbs or bouquet garni to your bouillon (parsley, carrot, thyme, bayleaf, peppercorns). At the end add a glass of white wine. Finish your sauce with a roux blanc like a white sauce. Add a little 35 per cent cream before serving.

CIVET OF RABBIT (or HARE)   Serves 6

1 rabbit-4-5 lb (2 kg)—
   6-12 months old
2 large onions
2 garlic cloves
1 carrot
Parsley sprigs
1 rib of celery

1 tbsp thyme, 6 cloves,
   4 bay leaves, 6 juniper
   berries, crushed
Salt, pepper
1 bottle red table wine
   (about 30 oz, 850 g)
1 tbsp tomato paste or
   1 diced ripe tomato

Roux
2 oz (50 g) butter
Garniture
10 small onions
10 small mushrooms

2 oz (50 g) flour

5 oz (150 g) 'lardons', diced
   salt pork, lightly
   browned and rendered

Cut rabbit into pieces of 4 legs, rump into 5 sections. Put in jar or crock add and mix with coarsely chopped vegetables and spices, cover with red wine and let stand for 48 hours in cold place. Put butter in casserole or pan and sauté the onions, mushrooms, salt pork. Take the vegetables out and put aside. Sauté rabbit in the same pan, brown lightly and put aside. Sauté and brown the well-drained vegetables—add flour, tomato paste and mix well. Add the wine and bring to boil. Add rabbit and let simmer for 1½-2 hours or until tender. The wine must cover the rabbit. If not, add more wine, chicken stock or simply water.

When cooked put rabbit pieces on a serving dish, add heated garniture, pour sauce over it (through a sieve) sprinkle parsley— serve with medium egg noodles. If served with noodles no other vegetable is required.

‾ This recipe can be used for a variation of coq au vin or cubed beef, (Boeuf Bourguignon) or larger game like moose or deer, in the latter case you would use the shoulder and the less tender pieces.

TOURTIERE (French Canadian Meat Pie)   *Serves 4*

1 lb (450 g) fairly lean pork, minced   ⅓ cup chopped celery
2 small chopped onion   ¾ cup water
1 tsp salt   ⅓ cup finely chopped potatoes
½ tsp mixed herbs   1 pinch cinnamon
¼ tsp cloves   One 9 inch pie.

Mix all the ingredients and boil for 30-40 minutes. Let cool. Pour into pie crust and cover with same. Bake until golden brown at 200°C (400°F) Gas Mark 6. Serve hot with home-made fruit sauce, ketchup or pickles. This is an excellent dish for cooler days. It can be reheated or even frozen and served several days later.

Basically, French Canadian cuisine uses a lot of pork or pork products. This is mostly due to tradition imposed on early settlers by the very harsh climate and the impossibility to get meat other than pork (mostly salt pork brought in by ships) and game.

This liking for pork still exists to a certain extent, especially in the country. This peculiarity is accompanied for the same reason by a great liking for sugar and sugar products. For most Canadians a pie can never be sweet enough. As a result, the Indians, who first were aware of the sugar content of the maple sap, were soon not the only ones to take advantage of this natural resource. Maple syrup and maple sugar products are therefore very popular.

MAPLE SYRUP PIE   *Serves 4*

1 cup maple syrup   2 tbsp butter
⅓ cup water   ⅓ cup nuts (grenoble or
3 tbsp cornstarch   pecan)
                           Your favourite pie crust

Bring to boil maple syrup and water. Mix cornstarch with a little water, pour into boiling syrup, stir well until mixture is nice and smooth. Add butter and nuts according to taste. Pour into 9-inch pie dish, cover with same pie crust. Make small cuts on top. Bake at 190°C (375°F) Gas Mark 5 for 20-30 minutes.

In Kenora, Ontario, we met Bruce and Vicky Vodrey who own the Norman Hotel and Vicky gave me the following recipe which goes well with poultry and, if wild rice is not easy to obtain, long grain ordinary rice is a good substitute.

WILD RICE AND MUSHROOM CASSEROLE   *Serves 4*

²/₃ cup Pure Canadian Wild Rice
3 cups boiling water,
½ tsp salt
¼ cup chopped onion
1 cup fresh mushrooms, sliced
2 tbsp butter
1 tbsp flour

1 cup beef bouillon or
  1 cube dissolved in
  1 cup boiling water
½-¾ tsp salt
¹/₈ tsp pepper
¼ cup slivered or thinly
  sliced almonds

Cook the rice in the 3 cups boiling water and ½ teaspoon salt. Sauté onion and mushroom in butter. Blend in the flour and the cooked roux. Add bouillon, cooking until smooth and thickened. Add salt and pepper and cooked rice. Turn into a buttered 1-quart (1 litre) casserole dish. Sprinkle with almonds. Cover and bake at 180°C (350°F) Gas Mark 4 for 30 minutes.

Serve with cooked duck and orange sauce.

TRIFLE   *Serves 6*

This recipe comes from Lunenburg.

Cut 2 plain sponge layers in strips and spread generously with jam (strawberry or raspberry) or jelly (currant or grape). Place one quarter of jam strips criss-cross in bowl and cover completely with chilled custard sauce. Repeat until cake and custard are used, ending with custard. Chill overnight or at least 8 hours. Top with whipped cream and sprinkle with finely chopped nuts.

6 tbsp flour
1 cup sugar
¹/₈ tsp salt
4 eggs

4 cups milk
2 tsp vanilla essence
Plain sponge layers
5 oz (150 ml) whipped cream
Chopped nuts

Mix flour, sugar, salt. Beat eggs slightly and add. Scald milk and gradually add. Cook over hot water, stirring constantly until mixture thickens and coats the spoon. Cool. Add the vanilla (or/and brandy, sherry or rum). Chill.

It goes without saying that the steaks in Calgary are mouth-watering but they also have what they call 'Calgary's Official Dish' which is White Hatter Stew:

WHITE HATTER STEW   *Serves 6*
Filling

2½ lb (1 kg) beef rump or
   other suitable stew
   meat, cubed
2 large onions, chopped
⅕ of 28 oz can plum
   tomatoes (½ cup)

2 tbsp flour
Oil, salt and pepper to taste
½ tsp monosodium glutamate
⅓ tsp paprika
1 tsp Worcestershire sauce

Top Crust

4 cups flour
8 tbsp margarine
⅔ tbsp baking powder

1 egg
1 cup milk
Pinch of salt

'Bouquet Garni' consisting of 2 bay leaves, few peppercorns, thyme, parsley stalks, all wrapped in a piece of cheesecloth.
1 cup whole medium mushrooms   1 quart (1 litre) good brown
½ cup or more beer (optional)   stock or diluted brown gravy

Heat oil in pan until slightly smoking. Arrange meat cubes in it and put into preheated oven at 200°C (400°F) Gas Mark 6 for 15 minutes, shaking pan occasionally so meat can brown on all sides. Add onions, pepper, monosodium glutamate, paprika and sprinkle with flour. Continue cooking another 20 minutes, stirring occasionally. Add tomatoes, bouquet garni, stock, Worcestershire sauce, beer, and cover the pan. Reduce heat to 150°C (300°F) Gas Mark 2 and continue cooking until meat is tender. Then arrange stew in individual casseroles. In the meantime prepare biscuit crust.

Mix dry ingredients well, work in margarine. Beat egg with milk. Make a well in the dry mixture, pour in the liquid and mix together lightly until one lump of dough is obtained. Roll out on floured board to ¼″ (6 mm) thickness. Cut out pastry covers the same size as your casseroles. Place dough over stew in casseroles and seal tightly in order to keep all flavour in. Brush tops with milk and bake 15 minutes in hot oven.

SCALLOPED LOBSTER   *Serves 4*
This recipe comes from New Brunswick.

1½ cups lobster meat
1 cup soft breadcrumbs
1 cup top milk or thin cream
1 egg, well beaten
2 tbsp melted butter or margarine

½ tsp prepared mustard
1 tsp lemon juice
Few drops onion juice
½ tsp salt, pepper if desired
To decorate: crumbs

Mix in order given. (Crabmeat, fresh or canned, may be substituted for the lobster meat.) Put into greased baking dish and cover with buttered crumbs. Bake for 30 minutes in moderate oven 180°C (350°F) Gas Mark 4.

LOBSTER BISQUE   *Serves 4*
This recipe comes from New Brunswick.
1 tablespoon chopped onion boiled in small amount of water until tender. Add to this ½ pint (¼ litre) milk and 1 small can evaporated milk and butter the size of an egg. Add 2 cups fresh lobster, salt, pepper, dash onion salt. Serve piping hot.

Tea and coffee are great favourites in Canada but probably tea wins by a short head. It certainly does in Victoria and if you ask where you could buy the best tea in the island the answer would be Murchie's. The Murchie's store is not hard to identify as its front is a replica of No. 10 Downing Street. John Murchie's dedication to blending and marketing techniques have paid off handsomely in a number of ways. Five years ago when Queen Elizabeth stopped overnight in Vancouver en route to Australia a gift pack of 24 teas was made up to go aboard the royal yacht for its Pacific journey. Murchie now has permission to retail a gold box of tea as the store's select 'Royal Canadian' package. In 1974 the firm took delivery of what is believed to be the largest single shipment of select Darjeeling teas to enter any port in North America. Worth $100,000 the shipment was packaged for sale as the 1974 vintage; the labels on the tins even indicate which of Darjeeling's 138 tea gardens produced the product inside.

Today in Victoria, tea and Murchie's are synonymous. The city is still the centre of a cult of tea worshippers. Government workers do not stop for 'coffee breaks'—they disappear for a 'spot of tea'. Afternoon high tea in Victoria is still fashionable and more traditional than anything experienced in London since the turn of the century. The best silverware and white napkins are still there—as are the ladies with gloves and flowered hats. However, you are likely to lose sight of them in the crowd of blue jeans, sneakers and beards which patiently line up for a 'cuppa'.

Canadian wine deserves to be better known and you will not regret trying it. Much of its source is from highly prized French hybrid strains such as pinot noir and other classic European wine grapes which thrive along the Lake Ontario shoreline of the Niagara Peninsula. Starting from the outskirts of Hamilton, 25,000 acres (10,117 hectares) of vineyards lie along the route, through Grimsby, Lincoln, Vineland, Jordan, Thorold, St Catharines, Niagara-on-the-Lake and Niagara Falls. The quality of soil combined with the long season, which continues until late into the autumn, provides growing conditions unequalled anywhere else in Canada and similar to those in Europe. A total of forty-five distinct grape varieties are now grown commercially in Niagara.

The annual Niagara Grape and Wine Festival, similar to the vendanges in Europe, is held in the town of St Catharines when the grapes are gathered in September. During the festival you can get tickets from the Tourist Bureau to join in winery tours. There are arts and crafts shows, wine-tasting parties in the wine gardens and bus tours throughout the area. The highlight is the crowning of the Niagara Grape and Wine Festival Queen at the Queen Coronation Ball. St Catharines is the main town of the Niagara Peninsula because of the nearby Welland ship canals which take sea-going vessels round the Niagara Falls. The newest canal passes through vineyards and peach orchards within the town boundaries.

Should you buy some of Bright and Company's wine or champagne from a government liquor store do not be surprised if the shelves you are directed to, have the unusual names of 'Cold Duck' or 'Cold Duckling'. There is a Germanic reason for this name. Originally 'kalte ente' was a mixture of the last of the sparkling wines consumed at the end of a German festival: *'kalte ente'*—'the cold end'. The German word for duck is also *ente*—and as a pun the drink became known as 'kalte ente'—Cold Duck. Bright's Cold Duck was introduced in Canada in 1970—and twelve months later was a runaway best seller.

The introduction of Still Cold Duck, Cold Duck without the sparkle, was received with even greater enthusiasm. Now for weddings another sparkling wine is most popular, a type of champagne and its name is Cold Duckling!

You can get good sherries and ports. Indeed Bright's are specializing in the latter which is being drunk in increasing quantities by Canadians. Their special port for Queen Elizabeth's silver jubilee is an excellent one.

The connection between port and Newfoundland is well known and, like so many good things in life, came about by chance some three hundred years ago. In those piratical times a British merchant ship with a cargo of port wine from Oporto to London only managed to avoid a French privateer by heading for St John's.

The ship remained in the harbour throughout the winter, probably due to icebergs and inclement weather. She returned to London in the spring where it was discovered that the quality of the port had been greatly enhanced by its journey. Whether this was caused by the cold, moist air or the motion of the ship was not evident but the message was clear. Newman's Port has been carried to Newfoundland, aged in vaults there, and brought back to England ever since.

Spirits are as popular in Canada as in any other country, their speciality being rye whisky. The mixing of drinks also causes as much controversy as elsewhere, and the relative proportions of gin and dry vermouth to make a martini are always good for an argument. A story is told about this as follows.

A mountie was being issued with all his equipment to sally forth on his first assignment. The quartermaster helped him to check the items. When this was finished the Mountie was handed a small case. 'This is the most important thing you must carry with you where ever you go,' he was told. The Mountie opened the case and found a small bottle of gin and another of dry vermouth. He looked somewhat astonished and the quartermaster's eyes twinkled. 'I mean it,' he said, 'when you are trying to catch a criminal and you have been chasing him in the frozen north for weeks and your horse is dead and you've eaten your last rations you'll remember this case and you'll get it out thinking to yourself that at least you will die comfortably. You'll start to mix yourself a martini amid the snow drifts and sure as my name is Ebenezer Schultz, some guy will spring up from nowhere and say—"that's no way to mix a martini."'

INDEX